Rembrandt's
Nightwatch

Rembrandt's Nightwatch

The history of a painting

WILLEM HIJMANS

LUITSEN KUIPER

ANNEMARIE VELS HEIJN

A.W. Sijthoff – Alphen aan den Rijn

Production, design and picture research by Leo Verbeek, Nieuwkoop
Printed by De Lange/Van Leer B.V., Deventer
Plates by Rommerts & Van Santen B.V., Utrecht
Typesetting by Studiozetterij Eduard Bos, Rotterdam
Bound by Albracht B.V., Utrecht

With grateful acknowledgement of the assistance of:
The Amsterdam Historical Museum
The Historical and Topographical Atlas, Municipal Archives, Amsterdam
The Doelen Hotel, Amsterdam
Greet and Han van Hagen, Nieuwkoop
The Hesterman Family, Rijswijk
The Mauritshuis, The Hague
The Amstelkring Museum, Amsterdam
The Rembrandthuis, Amsterdam
The Netherlands Press Museum, Amsterdam
The Netherlands Historical Navigation Museum, Amsterdam
The Atlas van Stolk Foundation, Rotterdam
The Rijksprentenkabinet, Rijksmuseum, Amsterdam
Translated by Patricia Wardle
Illustration opposite the title-page:
Rembrandt, *Self portrait,* 1628

ISBN 90 218 2358 6

Contents

6

Authors' Preface

On 14 September 1975 Rembrandt's *Nightwatch* – one of the world's most famous paintings – was seriously damaged by being slashed with a knife. By 4 June 1976 it had been completely repaired and thoroughly restored and could be put on display again for visitors to the Rijksmuseum. That act of violence and the subsequent restoration were the immediate stimuli behind the writing of this book.

Innumerable books have been published on Rembrandt and thus on the *Nightwatch* as well, so can yet another really add anything new? We believe it can, for precisely what has been lacking of recent years is an up-to-date book meant for the wide audience that is interested in the subject but not versed in art history. Many stories about Rembrandt that are still persistently going the rounds have been relegated in recent decades to the realm of beloved but quite unproven legend, while at the same time scholarly ideas on the subject of Rembrandt, his times, the *Nightwatch* and its restoration have been amended, amplified and improved.

This book is definitely not an academic study, but in it we have tried to recount for every admirer of the *Nightwatch* its plain, unvarnished history, freed from all superfluous and confusing embellishments. In other words, we have tried to set down the naked truth and the honest doubts as we understand them at the present moment.

Who was Rembrandt?

Rembrandt's education – influences on his work – his style – his situation as a painter around 1640 – his pupils

Rembrandt was born in Leiden on 15 July 1606. His father was a miller or, to put it more accurately, part-owner of the mill De Rijn ('The Rhine'), where malt was ground for breweries. He was one of the many people in the Republic of the United Netherlands who profited from the growth in prosperity and, notwithstanding their humble origins, also acquired greater prestige as a result of their increased wealth. Rembrandt, the youngest but one of nine children, was given an education appropriate to his father's standing. At the age of seven he went to the Latin School, where Latin grammar was the principal subject, along with the reading of such Roman authors as Cicero and Virgil. The quality of the education depended very much on the teachers, since there were no set programmes of education or examinations in those days.

As far as we know, Rembrandt's four brothers all learned a trade. Rembrandt himself, of course, became a painter. The choice of this calling was not so surprising for a boy from a tradesman's family in the seventeenth century as it might seem today, for it was not thought of as a question of vocation or talent. The general view at that time was that the craft of painting was one that anyone who had a bit of natural aptitude could learn by diligent study and a lot of practice. A throrough knowledge of the technical aspects was a primary requirement for a painter of any kind and a great deal of attention was also paid to it in the training of painters who were destined to become artists. Nor at that time was the calling unavoidably linked in people's minds with the financial insecurity that is now often regarded as an inevitable aspect of an artist's existence, since it offered just as good prospects of an adequate income as that of a craftsman like a carpenter or saddler. There was a great demand for paintings and the attitude of artists in those days was not such that they found it difficult to fit in with the wishes of their patrons. The idea that the creation of a work of art is a question of inspiration and thus something that the artist must carry out according to his own judgement, even if this might go against that of his patrons, was unknown to the artists of the early seventeenth century.

Molitaris etiam Leidensis filius magni fit, sed ante tempus – a great deal that is good is said of a Leiden miller's son, but it is somewhat premature – so wrote a Leiden law student, Aernout van Buchell, in 1628 in notes meant for a book on painting that never appeared. This is the first time that Rembrandt is mentioned as a painter, although Van Buchell does not actually refer to him by name.

The engraving on p.8 shows one of the original buildings of Leiden University at the time of its foundation in 1575.

Rembrandt was apprenticed to the Leiden painter Jacob van Swanenburch. He was also enrolled at Leiden University, but whether he really intended to study there is not known. It seems that many young men had themselves enrolled merely in order to share in the privileges which students enjoyed, such as exemption from paying the taxes on alcoholic drinks and from military service. That Van Swanenburch was but a mediocre artist will not have been detrimental to Rembrandt, for the first years of a painter's training were, after all, largely devoted to instruction in the technical aspects of the work: stretching canvases, planing panels, grounding canvases and panels, grinding pigments and mixing paint, making up varnish. It is thanks to that sound knowledge of the technical side that seventeenth-century paintings are often still in such excellent condition today.

It does nonetheless appear that after a while Rembrandt's aspirations went beyond what Van Swanenburch could teach him. He wanted to be a history painter. History painting was regarded as the highest branch of the art, higher than the painting of landscapes, portraits

The Prophetess Hannah, reading the Bible, painted by Rembrandt in 1631. It is often thought that Rembrandt's mother was the model for this painting, but there is no evidence for this.

Page 375 from the *Description of the City of Leiden* by the Leiden burgomaster J. Orlers, where an account of Rembrandt's life is given. The first edition of the book appeared as early as 1614 and Rembrandt was naturally not included in it. This is the second edition of 1641.

The Anatomy Lesson of Dr. Nicolaas Tulp, Praelector in Anatomy, painted by Rembrandt in 1632 on commission from the Amsterdam Surgeons's Guild.

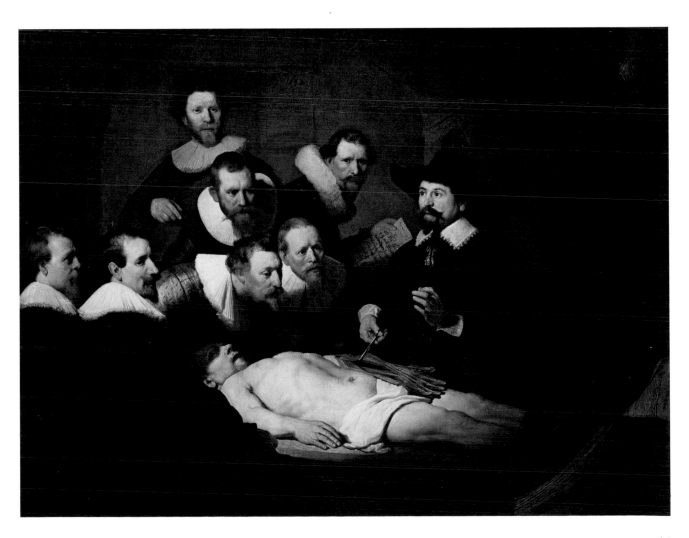

or scenes from daily life. It was concerned not only with the representation of subjects taken from history, but also with themes from mythology or the Bible. To be a history painter an artist had to have great powers of imagination, since he could not just borrow his depictions from what he saw around him.

In 1624, probably on the advice of the young Leiden painter Jan Lievens, Rembrandt went to Amsterdam to study under Pieter Lastman. Lastman (1583-1633) was an esteemed history painter. Moreover, as a young artist he had spent some years in Italy, in Venice and Rome, and his familiarity with Italian art lent him an even greater prestige. In Italy he had been able to get to know the work of the great artists of the Renaissance, Raphael, Michelangelo and Titian, and he had also participated in important new movements in painting, to which belonged the spectacular pictures produced by Caravaggio during those years.

Lastman did not make much use of Caravaggio's innovations in his own work, but he will undoubtedly have told his pupils about them

The old Reguliers Gate at Amsterdam.

D'oude REGULIERS Poorte t'Amsterdam.

12

and in Rembrandt's case his words certainly did not fall on deaf ears. Lastman himself, however, was more influenced by the work of the German artist Adam Elsheimer, who had managed in Rome to apply the rich colour and lively movement of Italian painting to pictures of small format. It was this style of painting that Lastman was still practising twenty or so years later when Rembrandt became his pupil. Although his pictures will certainly have appeared Italian in Dutch eyes, they were not really so, for they lacked the largeness of scale that is an essential feature of Italian painting. Lastman's *Entombment,* which as far as composition and colour are concerned is one of the most Italianate of his works, measures only 123 x 101 cm, while a similar Italian painting would easily run to around 250 x 200 cm. Thus Rembrandt's introduction to Italian art "at second-hand" was undoubtedly somewhat deficient. As far as is known, he only stayed with Lastman for six months before returning to Leiden. No paintings by him are known from his time with Lastman or the period before, since it was customary for pupils during their apprenticeship to assist with the paintings of their teachers or else for teachers to sell paintings by their pupils under their own names.

Rembrandt's paintings of 1625 and 1626 show that he had indeed realised his dream of becoming a history painter and it is also clear that he had learned a great deal from Lastman in this respect. His earliest pictures are full of figures, painted in bright colours on panels

Transport from place to place was effected for centuries by water. Every day dozens of barges plied the waterways, like the Haarlem passenger barge in this print.

Haerlemſe Iaegſchuyties

7.

People in the Netherlands were well informed about Italian art. Almost all important Italian paintings were reproduced in print form, Italian pictures often came up for sale on the Amsterdam art market and there were Italian works of art in Amsterdam collections. A well-known example is the splendid collection of the Spanish merchant, Alfonso Lopez, who lived in Amsterdam. It included Raphael's portrait of Baldassare Castiglione (now in the Louvre, Paris) and Titian's portrait of Ludovico Ariosto (now in the National Gallery, London). Rembrandt certainly saw these paintings and in the print collection he acquired over the years there were numerous prints after works by Raphael, Leonardo da Vinci, Titian, the Carracci and Michelangelo. These prints were, above all, important study material when it was required to take cognizance of the way in which the Italians represented figures and built up their compositions, but they lacked two important elements in Italian art: the scale of the pictures and their colour. Italian paintings meant for churches and palaces had the magnitude of scale that suited those large buildings, but it was a magnitude that was inconceivable to Dutch painters, whose pictures were primarily meant for the decoration of rooms in houses. The colour of many Italian paintings was also unfamiliar to Dutch eyes, especially when it came to frescoes, like those of Michelangelo in the Sistine Chapel or of Raphael in the Stanze in the Vatican palace. Rembrandt consciously (and probably unconsciously too) borrowed a great deal from Italian models. There was nothing reprehensible in the 17th century about taking over inventions and compositions by other painters into one's own pictures. It was even recommended, as long as it was done with good taste and one's own inventions and those of others formed a unified whole in the completed painting.

Detail of the *Disputa del Sacramento,* a fresco by Raphael in the Stanze of the Vatican palace in Rome.

A Scene from the Play *Gysbrecht van Aemstel,* a drawing by Rembrandt.

Caravaggio, *The Entombment of Christ*, 1603-4.

Caravaggio (1573-1610) had to endure a considerable amount of criticism of his paintings, which many people found too realistic to suit their taste. He took ordinary peasants or townsfolk as models for his pictures and that was considered unsuitable for artistic expressions in which, after all, beauty was a prime requirement. And it was certainly objectionable, people thought, that ordinary people should even represent saints. Caravaggio also heightened the effect of his compositions by a strong play of light and dark, chiaroscuro, and by painting the scenes without foregrounds, so that the spectator is actually directly involved in what is happening.

He was greatly admired by a number of Dutch painters who worked in Rome. In particular, some of the painters from Utrecht who spent time there became faithful followers of his style and thus came to be known as the Caravaggists. The most important representatives of this group are Hendrik Terbrugghen, Gerard Honthorst and Dirck van Baburen. In 1605-6 Caravaggio painted two pictures for the church of Santa Maria del Popolo: *The Conversion of St. Paul* and *The Crucifixion of St. Peter*. This church was just inside the gate through which travellers from the north entered Rome and it was for many Dutch painters their first introduction to the painting of that city. Moreover, the district in which the church stood was one where many painters from the north settled.

of generous size. But there is one very obvious difference between his work and that of his teacher. Lastman was in the habit of telling his stories by means of a large number of figures spread out over the whole width of the painting and arranged in such a way that it is not immediately clear where the most important part of the action is taking place. Rembrandt took the greatest pains to give his story form in a way that would be, above all, arresting, making all his figures concentrate their attention on the main events and "piling them up", so that all the emphasis fell on the principal action, the theme of painting. For this reason he soon abandoned the horizontal format that Lastman used in favour of an upright one, which offered

15

An Oriental Ruler on Horseback, a drawing by Rembrandt of 1625-6.

The Baptism of the Eunuch, painted by Pieter Lastman in 1620.

more possibilities for his method of composing.

In March 1976 the Aartsbisschoppelijk Museum in Utrecht bought a previously unknown painting by Rembrandt. It was done early in 1626 and its subject is the *Baptism of the Eunuch,* a story from the Acts of the Apostles, which tells how the Apostle Philip baptized the high official who was in charge of all the treasure of the Queen of Ethiopia. Lastman had also painted this subject several times. On one of his pictures, dated 1620, there is so much to be seen that one's attention is drawn not only to the main theme, the Eunuch being baptized by St. Philip, but also to groups of bystanders. Rembrandt went about it in a quite different way. In his picture all the attention is concentrated on the important event. The figures are somewhat awkwardly painted and the space relationships strikes one as rather improbable, but other paintings done by Rembrandt in the same year show that he very soon discovered how to overcome these problems.

In those first years in Leiden Rembrandt worked in close collaboration with Jan Lievens. They may possibly even have shared a studio. During that time, probably in 1629, the two painters were visited in Leiden by Constantijn Huygens, the secretary of the Stadholder, Prince Frederick Henry. Huygens, who was a great art-lover, devoted a passage to the visit in the Latin autobiography he was engaged in writing at that very time. He greatly admired the two artists, considering that, young though they still were, they had already

The Lamentation over and Entombment of Christ, a painting by Pieter Lastman in 1620.

reached the level of famous painters of the day and prophesying that they would soon even outstrip them. He also perceived the differences between them: Lievens painted large-scale works and was more inventive and daring than Rembrandt, but Rembrandt showed a taste and intensity of emotion in the depiction of his figures which Lievens did not possess. Rembrandt could achieve effects in small paintings that are often looked for in vain in larger ones. Huygens does express surprise that neither of them felt the need to make a visit to Italy in order to study the work of Raphael and Michelangelo there. But they said they were too busy to be able to do so and in any case there were plenty of fine Italian paintings to be seen in Holland too. They further remarked to Huygens "that, since kings and princes on this side of the Alps are collecting paintings with so much eagerness and devotion nowadays, one can see the best Italian works outside Italy and that what one would have great difficulty in tracking down there in all sorts of places is to be found heaped up here in more than sufficient quantity".

In those first years Rembrandt painted a large number of history

An Old Man, a drawing by Rembrandt of around 1629.

The Backgammon Players, a drawing by Rembrandt. The drawing probably shows a scene from the Parable of the Prodigal Son. The figures in the background represent a house of ill-fame in which the Prodigal son has got mixed up in bad company.

pieces, but it was nonetheless, his qualities as a portrait painter that were to determine his future. There was a great demand for portraits in the Republic. People's sense of their own dignity was on the increase now that the separation from Spain, and thus from the Catholic faith too, was steadily becoming more and more of an accomplished fact. And prosperity was on the increase too. So there was plenty of work for portrait painters, since the rich, free citizens of the Republic were only too pleased to have themselves immortalized. Rembrandt even attracted portrait commissions from Amsterdam.

When, in addition, he also got the chance to acquire for 1,000 guilders a share in an Amsterdam art-dealing business, that of Hendrick van Uylenburgh, and Van Uylenburgh probably also offered him a post at his school for painters, Rembrandt decided, in 1631, to move to Amsterdam for good. At Van Uylenburgh's school youngsters of good family were trained as copyists and the copies they made were then sold by Van Uylenburgh via his art-dealing business. It may be that paintings by Rembrandt were copied at the school too.

One of the first important commissions Rembrandt acquired in

Rembrandt's surname, Van Rijn, was derived from his father's mill, which was called *De Rijn* because it stood on the arm of the Rhine at Leiden known as the Old Rhine. In fact, however, Rembrandt himself never actually used this surname. In his Leiden period he called himself Rembrandt Harmensz(oon = son of Harmen) and he signed his paintings with RH (Rembrandt Harmenszoon) or RHL (Rembrandt Harmensz. of Leiden. In Amsterdam he used only his first name, Rembrandt. The letters he wrote to Constantijn Huygens in 1636 an 1639 are also signed simply with Rembrandt. In the 17th century surnames still often served as a sort of nickname to make a distinction between people with the same first name and such a surname by no means always became a family name that passed on to the next generation. Rembrandt evidently felt that someone with such an uncommon first name as his had no need whatsoever of a surname, although in official documents he is always conscientiously referred to as Rembrandt van Rijn. His unusual first name may perhaps have come from his mother's family. Her grandmother was called Reijmptje, which could be another form of the same name. By a coincidence, the father of Rembrandt's wife, Saskia, had the first name of Rombertus, which is another form of the same name.

The Baptism of the Eunuch, a painting by Rembrandt of 1626. This is one of the earliest known paintings by Rembrandt. At the bottom on the right are inscribed the letters RF *(Rembrandt Fecit,* Rembrandt made it) and the date 1626.

Judas Returning the Thirty Pieces of Silver, Judas, overcome by remorse, giving back to the Pharisees the money he had received for betraying Christ. Rembrandt painted this picture in 1629 (p.18).

A Musical Party, a painting by
Rembrandt of 1626. It is thought that
the young man with the harp may be
Rembrandt himself.

The Flute player, an etching by
Rembrandt of 1642.

Amsterdam came from the Surgeons' Guild, for which he was asked
to make a painting of the anatomy lesson of Dr. Nicolaes Tulp.
Anatomy lessons were rare occurrences, since dissections were
allowed to be carried out only once a year and then on the corpse
of a condemned criminal. In January 1632 Nicolaes Tulp gave a
public lesson on the physiology of the arm. In the group portrait
he made of this event Rembrandt proved that he knew how to apply
all the intensity of emotion that Huygens had so admired in his
history pieces to portraits as well. The keen interest of the surgeons
in what Dr. Tulp is saying can be read in their faces.
Sometimes Rembrandt also adopted the costumes of his history
paintings in portraits. The dressing up of models in bizarre costumes
was less strange and unusual than it might seem, for those costumes
contained allusions to certain Biblical or literary texts and they thus
gave the portraits a deeper significance which, alas, can by no means
always be tracked down nowadays.

At the very moment of Amsterdam's explosive expansion, a burst dike brought about the destruction of the village of Houtewael or Oetewael which lay close to the boundary of 17th-century Amsterdam, roughly where the Oranje Nassau barracks stands today. The village was never rebuilt for Amsterdam appropriated the land for the extension of the city.

History painting itself continued to exert its hold on Rembrandt in Amsterdam, just as it had in Leiden. He made a great many painting of stories from the Bible, but this was probably not primarily because he himself was exceptionally religious. Whether he was really a believing Christian is not known, but it is certainly clear that he was always greatly fascinated by Bible stories for the reason that they often centre on human emotion. It is a striking fact that he mostly did not just adopt the form that had become traditional for many Bible stories, for it seems well-nigh certain that he invariably read the story for himself and then tried to find a way of depicting it so that the spectator could participate in the emotions involved.

Fishermen on the Amstel near Amsterdam.

21

The portrait of the wealthy Amsterdam merchant Nicolaes van Bambeeck painted by Rembrandt in 1641.

A Study for an Adoration of the Kings, a drawing by Rembrandt of around 1638.

Rembrandt was greatly admired for his history paintings. Constantijn Huygens wrote in glowing terms about his *Judas Returning the Thirty Pieces of Silver,* painted in 1629: "His gesture, the expression of his face, the torn garment, the clasped hands, his attitude, everything in this one figure expresses grief and remorse. The painters of Antiquity, Protogenes, Apelles and Parrhasios, would certainly never have been able to imagine what this beardless miller's son has been able to express in a single figure!" Huygens saw to it that Rembrandt got the commission to paint a series of paintings of the Passion of Christ for Prince Frederick Henry and Rembrandt delivered the five pictures between 1634 and 1639.

Rembrandt was praised by his fellow-artists too. The Leiden painter Philips Angel spoke admiringly of his *Samson's Wedding Feast* of 1638 in an address delivered to the painters' guild in Leiden.

What pleased Angel most in that picture was the way Rembrandt had shown his knowledge of history. Rembrandt has depicted the guests

Agatha Bas, the wife of Nicolaes van Bambeeck, likewise painted by Rembrandt in 1641.

at the wedding feast not sitting, but reclining, "for the Ancients", said Angel, "used beds on which they lay and they did not sit at table in the way we do now, but reclined leaning on their elbows, as is still customary in those lands under the Turks, the which he has shown very nicely".

In his first years in Amsterdam Rembrandt lived in Hendrick Uylenburgh's house and it was probably there also that he met Uylenburgh's cousin Saskia from Friesland. She was an orphan of good family. Her father had several times been burgomaster of Leeuwarden and he had left his eight children a tidy inheritance. On 22 July 1634 Rembrandt and Saskia were married in the Reformed Church at St. Annaparochie in Friesland. A year before that, on the occasion of their betrothal, Rembrandt had made a drawing of her, on which he wrote that it was a portrait of Saskia. It is the only portrait known for certain to be of her, but the same face can still often be recognized on paintings Rembrandt made

Three studies of heads, for a painting of the Supper at Emmaus, a drawing by Rembrandt of around 1633-4.

after 1635. Sometimes he had just used her as a model for a history piece, sometimes he had painted a real portrait of her. Rembrandt and Saskia also continued to live in Van Uylenburgh's house for a little while after their marriage, but in 1635 they moved to Nieuwe Doelenstraat and in 1639 to a house on the Binnenamstel. In 1639 they moved yet again to a large house on Sint Anthonies Breestraat and this was no rented house, but one Rembrandt himself had bought.

He had in the meantime acquired so many pupils that he had been obliged to rent a warehouse on Bloemgracht in order to accommodate them all. In the warehouse he had little rooms screened off, so that each pupil had a place of his own. Rembrandt then regularly went the rounds to give them instruction. By no means all of his pupils are known to us by name and certainly not all of them will later have become more or less well-known painters. Some important pupils of the years 1632 to 1640 are Jacob Backer, Ferdinand Bol, Govert Flinck and Gerbrandt van den Eeckhout. It was customary for pupils to pay their teachers an annual fee of 100 guilders, for which they got board and lodging as well as painting lessons. One of Rembrandt's biographers, Arnoud Houbraken, tells us that Rembrandt certainly earned around 2,500 guilders a year from his pupils.

Rembrandt's position in Amsterdam was now established and commissions poured in. He became a respected customer at sales, where he bought prints, curios and also paintings by other artists. Perhaps he, just like many other painters, was engaged in art dealing himself, but it is certain that many of his purchases were meant for his studio. After all a painter, and certainly a history painter, needed

A portrait of Saskia by Rembrandt. Rembrandt wrote under the drawing: "this is a likeness of my wife when she was 21 years old on the third day after our betrothal, the 8th of June 1633".

A self portrait of Rembrandt with Saskia in the background.

a great deal of study material and material with which to furnish his paintings and clothe his models. From the financial standpoint Rembrandt was well able to afford these purchases. He had married a wife with a substantial dowry and he earned a lot of money from his pupils and his commissions for paintings. But when in 1639 he bought the house on Breestraat that accorded with his status, a big house with eight rooms, two kitchens and a large attic, he did not pay the purchase price of 13,000 guilders in a single lump sum. On the day of the conveyance, 1 May 1639, he paid 1,200 guilders, on 1 November of the same year he had to pay the same amount again and a year later another 850 guilders. He was then allowed to pay off the rest over five or six years at an interest rate of 5 percent. The

Samson's Wedding Feast, a story from the Old Testament, Judges 14:10-18. During his wedding feast Samson gave the guests a difficult riddle, but his wife was later to give away the answer to them. Rembrandt painted this picture in 1638.

first payment was probably made with the money he received, after lengthy insistence from Constantijn Huygens, for two paintings in the series for Frederick Henry, a sum of 1,200 guilders. He would have liked to have been paid 1,000 guilders for each painting, but the Stadholder and his secretary evidently considered that to be too much.

Around 1640, then, Rembrandt was one of the most esteemed painters in Amsterdam. In the field of history painting he had no equals, and as a portrait painter he was a match for such established names as Thomas de Keyser and Bartholomeus van der Helst. No wonder that his name sprang to mind in 1639-40 when the militiamen of the *Kloveniersdoelen* drew up their ambitious plan for the decoration of their Guildhall.

The house in Sint Anthonies Breestraat (now Jodenbreestraat) that Rembrandt bought in 1639 was built in 1606. In 1608 it became the property of the Antwerp wine-merchant Pieter Belten and it was from his heirs that Rembrandt bought it. They asked a purchase price of 13,000 guilders. It was quite a wide house, with a step-gable. The roof was aligned parallel to the street and the back part of the house was built at right-angles to it. In Rembrandt's time, or shortly before, two rooms were built one above the other over the inner courtyard of the house and at the same time the stair case that had previously been built out into the courtyard was moved to the back premises.

At the beginning of the 17th century Breestraat was a fashionable area, but that altered somewhat during the course of the century with the completion of the concentric belt of the Herengracht, Keizersgracht and Prinsengracht, for many rich people moved there. When Rembrandt went to live in Breestraat in 1639 his neighbour on the left was the merchant Salvador Rodrigues. Next door on the right lived the portrait-painter Nicolaes Eliasz. Hendrick van Uylenburgh, in whose house Rembrandt had lived earlier on, also lived in Breestraat. Obliquely opposite Rembrandt's house was that of the writer and publisher Menasseh ben Israel, who was also rabbi of the synagogue.

In 1659 Rembrandt was forced to sell the house as a result of being declared insolvent. It then fetched 11,000 guilders. Shortly afterwards it was radically altered into two houses. An extra storey was added on and the façade was altered.

In 1906, the 300th anniversary of Rembrandt's birth, the municipality of Amsterdam bought the house. The following year a Rembrandthuis Foundation was set up. It took the house over from the municipality and drew up plans for its installation as a museum. The house was restored, the old arrangement of the inside being reconstructed as far as possible. It was decided not to restore the façade to its old form as that would be too drastic an alteration, but the second front door was removed.

The Rembrandthuis museum was opened in 1911. In it were exhibited etchings and drawings by Rembrandt and paintings by his contemporaries. In 1974 extensive restoration work was needed, because the house was threatened with subsidence or even collapse as a result of the metro building activities. The restored Rembrandthuis was reopened to the public in 1975.

Rembrandt's house in Jodenbreestraat as it appeared in 1867 (left).

The Rembrandthuis in 1976.

The Omval, the Amstel near
Amsterdam at the point where the
circular canal of the Diemermeer
comes out into the river. The piece of
land between the Amstel and the
Diemermeer is called the Omval.
An etching of 1645 by Rembrandt.

A polder landscape painted by Jan van
Goyen in 1644.

The city on the Amstel

origins − explosive growth between 1580 and 1650 − social relationships − government − commerce and shipping

In the beginning there was a virtually inaccessible stretch of wilderness, of peat bog and marsh, separating the domains of the Counts of Holland and the bishops of Utrecht. Between the years 1000 and 1200 the area was gradually made into more or less habitable and cultivable land by means of peat-cutting and reclamation which produced a landscape full of little straight canals that drained into the small natural streams that had flowed there for centuries. Of these the Amstel is the broadest. It flows into the IJ, an arm of the brackish Zuiderzee and this meant that if the land on the sea side were to be made usable, the sweet water would

Map of the Amstelland, 1625, by Balthazar Floris.

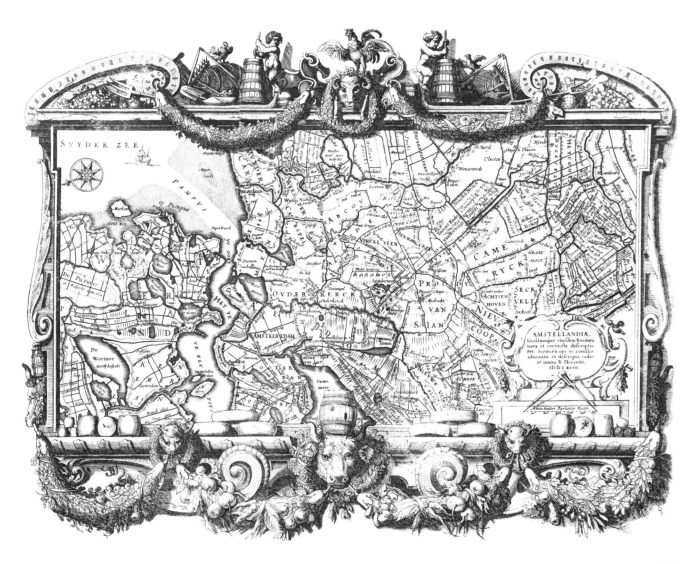

have to be held back by a dam. This was done about the middle of the thirteenth century, when a dam was built and people settled round it in simple wooden houses, the name Amsterdam meaning dam in the Amstel. On 27 October 1275 the settlement was granted exemption from tolls by Floris V, Count of Holland. Exactly when it obtained its urban charter is not known, but it must have been around 1306. It was then the last in the line of the numerous other cities in Holland, but a few centuries later it was to be the first. For that little city proved to be strategically situated on an exceptionally favourable spot for international trade. At the beginning of the fourteenth century ships from the locality were already sailing to the ports of Germany, Sweden and the Baltic to buy German beer and Baltic amber in exchange for herring, Rhine wine and Dutch cloth, a trade carried on by sturdy seafarers who managed to break the monopoly of the powerful Hanseatic League. Evidently Amsterdammers were troublesome, strong-willed types right from the very start.

The city grew rapidly. By the end of the fifteenth century it had around

Bird's Eye View of Amsterdam, a print made in 1544 after a painting of 1536 by Cornelis Anthonisz. The drainage canals in the area around Amsterdam are clearly visible on this map.

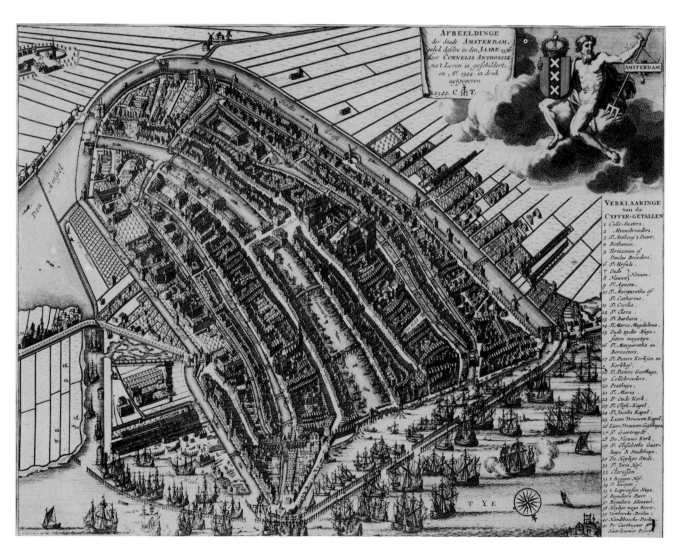

30

still remained tens of thousands balancing on a razor's edge: today a bit of money for bread and beer, tomorrow beggary. And what that meant for many of them was signing on with a ship bound for the East, North or West and taking the chance of being one of the one in eight who came back from such a voyage which often took several years. The other seven were drowned or killed or died of dysentery, scurvy or syphilis. And that one in eight, was he rich when he came back? Not a bit of it. It was the merchant-shipowner or merchant-captain trading at his own risk who raked in the profits. And so before the winter's end the crewmen were crowding round the harbour once more in order to get a chance to sail off again for months or years on end in cramped, stinking quarters for a pittance and mouldy ship's victuals. They sailed, so we are told by an nine thousand inhabitants and a century later, when various industries such as shipbuilding, soap-making and cloth-weaving had grown up, around 35,000. Amsterdam's economy flourished during that period, in spite of disastrous fires, periods of severe starvation resulting from unprecedented price rises and epidemics of cholera and plague. Then, at the end of the sixteenth and in the first half of the seventeenth century, the city "exploded". It literally burst out of its old walls and when Rembrandt went to live there around 1631, it numbered 115,000 inhabitants and there was building going on on all sides: new canals, new streets and alleys and thousands of houses. It was without doubt a rich city, at any rate for the rich. That same year the "list of the two-hundredth penny" (a property tax of a half per cent) included the names of four thousand people with a capital of a thousand guilders or more. In addition there was a very wealthy group with more than a hundred thousand guilders and one Croesus with a cool half million, the merchant Jacob Poppen.

But in those days too people managed to dodge taxes or pull the wool over tax officials' eyes, often enough with the latters' connivance. And even if there had really been not four but ten thousand rich people with a thousand or more guilders and even if there were some tens of thousands who could make a comfortable living as retail tradesmen, craftsmen or in the intellectual professions, there emblematic print of the early seventeenth century, "to all the principal Peoples on the face of the earth, each with its most excellent merchandise".

Since unity is strength, they generally sailed under the auspices of one of the three great trading companies that existed in the Republic in the first half of the seventeenth century. The oldest of the three was the United East India Company, which was set up in 1602 with the aid of the polished diplomacy of Johan van Oldenbarnevelt, after much negotiation between various smaller companies engaged in far flung trade. The East India Company had the monopoly for

Johan van Oldenbarnevelt is one of the most famous Dutch statesmen of the Golden Age. He lived from 1547 to 1619, when he was beheaded on the basis of very far-fetched charges. After making many journeys abroad, he became Grand Pensionary of the Court of Holland. One of the first to set the finances of Holland in order, he gave the economy a great boost by, among other things, the foundation of the Dutch East India Company and the West India Company.

Piet Heyn (1577-1629) went to sea at an early age, first in the service of the Dutch East India Company and later in that of the West India Company. He eventually rose to be Admiral of the Fleet. His best-remembered feat of arms was the capture of the Spanish silver fleet in the Bay of Matanzas on 8 and 9 September 1628.

the Netherlands on trade with all areas east of the Cape of Good Hope. Its ships sailed to India, the Dutch East Indies (present-day Indonesia), Ceylon, Formosa, China and Japan and it set up fortified factories all over this area, "pacified" (*i.e.* harassed and subdued) the local populace, should they happen to be so insolent as to fail to fall in with the wishes of the hard-bitten Dutch shipowners, and carried away millions of guilders' worth of rare Oriental goods.

Because people thought, following the logic of the sixteenth century atlases, that it ought als to be possible to get to "India" - the collective name applied to virtually every country inhabited by non-whites – via the Arctic, a Northern Company also came into being. After Heemskerk and Barentsz' futile attempts to find a north-east passage, Holland had lost an illusion, but she had gained a company that was to be engaged for half a century in whaling, mainly round the coasts of Greenland and Spitzbergen. This company died an inglorious death in the year of Rembrandt's *Nightwatch,* but whaling was still carried on on an individual basis.

Plan of Amsterdam, around 1650, by Claes Visscher. The first part of the concentric belt of three canals has already been built.

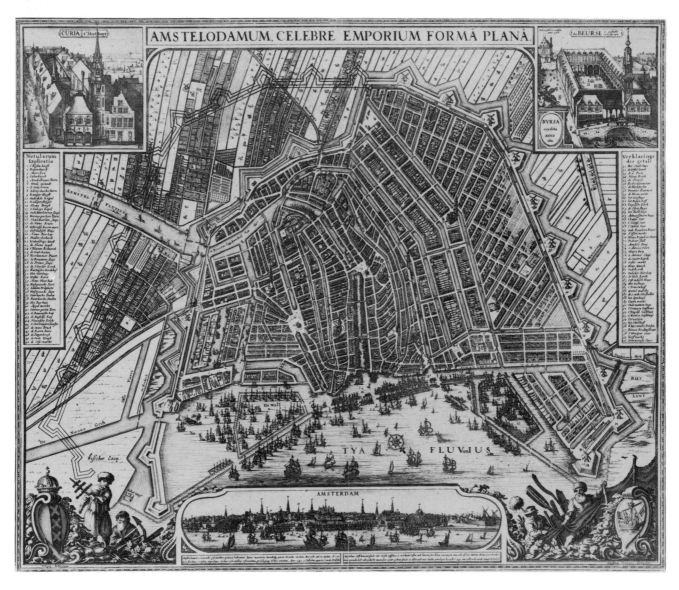

The third part of the world, the West, really did merit a company of its own and the West India Company was set up in 1621. It was very soon discovered that the founding of colonies in North and South America was a highly lucrative undertaking, especially if the work on them could be done by slaves captured or recruited in Africa, and that large-scale privateering (which was regarded as a perfectly normal weapon in the economic warfare of these days) could bring more money into the coffers than the laborious carrying home of pepper, cinnamon or porcelain from the East. Officially the West India Company continued to exist until 1674. Its greatest achievement in Dutch eyes was Piet Heyn's capture of the Silver Fleet, but that was, after all, a feat of arms that yielded such an unimaginably vast sum of money, that Dutch schoolchildren still learn a song about it to this very day. The spoils on that occasion comprised 177,000 pounds of silver, 66 pounds of gold, 1,000 pearls, two million guilders' worth of cochineal (the basis of carmine red, among other things), eight tons of indigo, three tons of silk, 37,375 skins, stocks of musk and amber and much more besides.

But what about trade within Europe itself? This continued to be the most important, certainly after the appearance on the high seas of the "flute", a new, very long and fast ship with what in those days was an unprecedentedly large carrying capacity. Thus the Baltic in particular continued to be full of Dutch ships which sold their exotic wares there, carrying off in exchange grain and timber, two commodities in very short supply at home.

The siege of 's Hertogenbosch in 1629 was one of Prince Frederick Henry's most important successes in the struggle against Spain. This picture by Paulus van Hilligaert was painted in 1629. In the left foreground can be seen Frederick Henry, Ernst Casimir of Nassau and Frederick V, the Elector of Brandenburg.

A "receipt" from the Dutch East India Company for the financing of voyages overseas. These receipts are the first printed shares in the world.

The navigators Jacob van Heemskerk (1567-1607) and Willem Barentsz, (1555-97) acquired fame through their attempt to find a passage to India via the Arctic. Their third expedition resulted in the celebrated winter spent in Nova Zembla in 1596-7. Both of them survived this experience, but Barentsz died of exhaustion on the voyage back to Holland in the early summer of 1597.

The meeting place of the Commissioners for Maritime Affairs on the "Grindstone Market", where millstones were sold. The building was also a Militia Guardhouse. St. Nicholas' Church now stands on approximately the same site, opposite the Central Station.

These trading activities governed the appearance of the city. The harbour was continually in need of extension, a corn exchange and a general stock exchange came into being and there was also an exchange bank and numerous work places resembling factories. The streets were full of stalls where street-traders offered every possible kind of ware for sale (the Amsterdam fishwifes were the most famous of them all in the city's history on account of their generosity to poor children). There were street-musicians too and performances put on by strolling comedians and wild-beast tamers. The crafts continued at this period to be strictly organized in the old way, *i.e.* in guilds dating from the Middle Ages, of which one had to be a member if one wanted to be able to practise such trades as that of baker, butcher, surgeon, cobbler or bookseller. Thus the painters were members of the Guild of St. Luke which, like the other guilds, was governed by chosen officials who had in their turn to render accountability and responsibility to the burgomasters, for it was the burgomasters who fixed wages and prices and had the quality of the work controlled.

And indeed that was only one part of the work done by the burgomasters, who were in fact the absolute rulers of the city. Each year a new board of four burgomasters was elected, not by the whole population, of course, but by the small group of former burgomasters, aldermen and ex-aldermen. They had the right of appointment to virtually all public offices, though the council, a sort of city parliament with little real power, could act as an advisory body. It goes without

EERSTE DEEL.

Wacht huys of Camer vande E E Heeren vant water-recht

Verscheyde Schepen en Gesichten van Amstelredam, Amstelodami Apud
Naer 't leven afgetekent en opt Cooper gebracht, door Reinier Nooms, alijas zeeman. Dancker: Danckerts.

A Quack Doctor, a drawing by Rembrandt of around 1637.

The Breach in St. Anthony's Dyke near Houtewael on 5 March 1651, a painting by W. Schellincks. In the background the skyline of Amsterdam.

A debenture issued in 1638 by the Polder Board of Lekdijk Bovendams. Eighty guilders is still paid out every year on this debenture.

saying that there thus very soon grew up a city aristocracy, in which the notables often kept the ball rolling between themselves. The Amsterdam patriciate, which was mainly based on wealth, generally ruled the city well, but it was far from democratic.

In a turbulent city like Amsterdam the sheriff and magistrates had their hands full. It was, for example, swarming with beggars, who, if they did not have written permission to beg, landed in the House of Correction (*Rasphuis,* later the Almshouse) where they were obliged to rasp brazilwood (a raw material for paint, among other things). And if they were beggarwomen or women of easy virtue, then they went to the *Spinhuis,* where they had to do spinning and sewing. All this served in fact as a public entertainment, for smug, respectable citizens could for a penny go in and have a look at what happened to "lazy and useless folk". More serious crimes were tried by the authorities in the town hall. Torture was the normal method of obtaining confessions and the punishments were banishment, branding, mutilation or hanging, this last being once again a public entertainment.

At this period, too, the city was responsible for the care of orphans and old people, often many hundreds of them. Large homes were set up for them, which were governed by regents. Here again it was evidently more blessed to give than to receive. The orphans and paupers were expected time and time again to eulogize the generosity of their regents with humble gratitude, but they were subjected to strict regimes – a state of affairs of which there can be no better

The City Orphanages for Boys and Girls in Amsterdam.

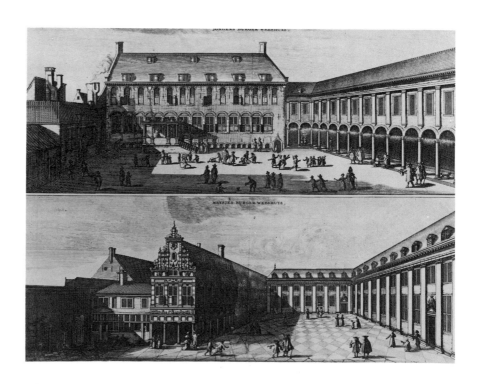

Etchings by Rembrandt. From 1613 on begging was officially forbidden in Amsterdam and many poor people at that time set about trying to earn a living as pedlars, rat-catchers or street musicians.

The Fishmarket, painted by Emanuel de Witte.

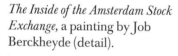

The Dam at Amsterdam with the Nieuwe Kerk, a painting by Jan van der Heyden.

The Inside of the Amsterdam Stock Exchange, a painting by Job Berckheyde (detail).

summing-up than that in the lines by P.C. Hooft that were carved into the gateway of the *Spinhuis:*

Schrik niet. Ik wreek geen quaet; maer dwing tot goet.
Straf is myn hant; maer lieflyk myn gemoet.
(Fear not. No evil I avenge. I enforce the better part.
Severe my hand may be, but loving is my heart.)

In short, strict order prevailed, imposed from above, and although disturbances were occasionaly caused in times of starvation by riots, they were speedily put down. There was order by day, when all was bustling activity, while the city clocks chimed the hours away, and order by night, when the nightwatchmen made their rounds, calling out the hours of darkness. And security reigned at the city gates and on the walls thanks to the watchfulness of vigilant civic guards who, in all the pride of their position as militiamen, completed the colourful picture of the Amsterdam we can still see in old paintings and prints.

The Amsterdam militia

three guilds: handbow archers, crossbow archers, arquebusiers – from guilds to militia – organization, arms and function

Like the other guilds the marksmen's guilds *(schuttersgilden)* came into being in the Middle Ages. The word *schutter* comes from *beschutten*, which means to protect, and that was indeed one of the most important tasks of the marksmen's guilds: to protect the city against threats from outside. In addition it was also their duty to march forth with their ruler to defend their country. To be a member of a markmen's guild was a question of status and money: only rich citizens of some standing could become marksmen, for they had to provide their own weapons and that involved a great deal of expense. In the course of time the duties of these guilds in respect of the defence of the country became ever more limited. Their rights only extended to the boundaries of their ruler's land and the more warfare came to be conducted over larger areas of territory the more

Seventeen Militiamen of the Handbow Archers' Doelen in 1613, a painting by Jan Tengnagel.

Arms used by both the army, and the militia: at the top, a round shield; below it on the ground, from top to bottom, a rapier, a sword and a dagger: in front, from left to right, a pike, a halberd and a spontoon; below, from left to right, a musket with support, a crossbow and a handbow; bottom of the page, a musket.

rulers gave preference to mercenary soldiers over the guilds. Originally there were two sorts of marksmen's guilds, which were distinguished by their weapons, the handbow and the crossbow. Crossbows were more substantial weapons than handbows and the arrows shot by them were heavier. They had to be placed on the ground and held in place by the archer's foot in order to be drawn, hence in Dutch they were given the name *voetboog* (footbow). They were more expensive than handbows and required a greater degree of skill. As a result of all this the Crossbow Archer's Guild traditionally enjoyed greater prestige than that of the Handbow Archers. During the reign of Charles V a third type of guild was set up: that of the arquebusiers *(kloveniers)*. They used heavy handguns with which bullets could be fired by means of gunpowder and which were originally called in Dutch *cloveren* (hence the word *kloveniers*). The word *clover* comes from the French *couleuvre*, a small type of gun. The places where targets were set up for the marksmen to practise were called *De Doelen* (the butts) and later on the whole guildhall of such a guild came to be called by this name.

After the Union of Utrecht in 1579, an alliance concluded between the provinces of the Netherlands in order that they could pursue the struggle against Spain as a united whole, the marksmen's guilds were completely reorganized. They were now put on a more military footing and from that moment on they were no longer a brotherhood of men of equal rank, but they became a militia with officers of various ranks placed over the men. Conscription was introduced and every man in a province between the ages of 18 and 60 was liable to military service. This liability was particularly strictly enforced in the towns and cities. The old *Doelen* of the handbow and crossbow archers and the arquebusiers continued to exist and the new militia companies were divided up between them.

The weaponry of the militiamen had indeed by that time become more or less uniform, the weapon in common use being the musket. It had been introduced into the Netherlands by the Spaniards around 1560, at which time it was still a heavy fire-arm that had to be propped up during aiming and firing on a long support with a forked end. Later on a lighter type weighing around four kilograms was

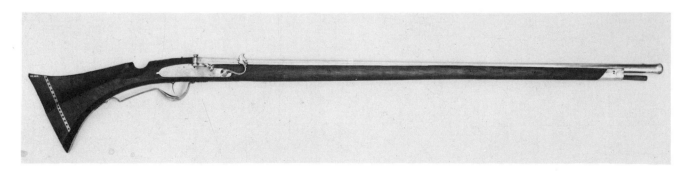

developed, which also came to be known as a musket eventually, though at first it was called a *roer*.

In the muskets of around 1640 the powder was ignited by a match (hence another English name for the gun, matchlock), but later on all sorts of other systems came to be used for this. For target practice a special simple type of fire-arm was used, the *doelroer*. Guns of this type were also carved on the stone tablet on the façade of the Amsterdam *Kloveniersdoelen*. The Amsterdam *Kloveniers* used a claw *(klauw)* as their symbol no doubt because of the similarity between the words *klover* and *klauw*, and this claw also appears on the stone tablet, as well as on the silver and glass of the *kloveniers*.

The militiamen were divided up into companies, each of which was recruited from a given area of the city. Around 1640 there were

The stone tablet from the façade of the old *Kloveniersdoelen*, the *Swygh Utrecht* Tower.

A chest from the *Kloveniersdoelen*, painted with the arms of officers or *Doelheren*.

Eulogy on the militiamen of the *Kloveniersdoelen*, published in 1659.

Portrait of Maria de Medicis, painted by Gerard van Honthorst in 1638.

twenty districts in Amsterdam and so there were twenty companies there too. Each company consisted of about 120 men commanded by a captain assisted by a lieutenant. Every company was further divided up into four corporalships of roughly thirty men. The high-ranking officers – the captains and lieutenants – were nominated for several years by the council. They belonged, naturally, to the regent class. The other officers – the ensigns, sergeants and corporals – were elected by the militiamen themselves. They belonged to the well-to-do citizenry. As the bearer of the distinguishing mark of his company the ensign had to measure up to very specific requirements: he had to be young, handsome and unmarried. The militia was governed by the *Doelheren,* the regents or governors, of each of the *Doelen,* while a master-at-arms looked after the finances.

Each militia company had three types of weapons. There were *rondassiers,* men armed with round shields, helmets and short swords, *piekeniers,* who wore helmets or hats and carried long pikes, and, finally, the *musketeers,* who handled the muskets. The high-ranking officers were armed with swords or rapiers and in addition they carried special insignia of rank, the captain a stick and the lieutenant a spontoon, a pike with a short shaft. The ensigns and sergeants also carried swords, while the sergeants had a halberd as a further distinguishing mark. In general the aims of the militia had much in common with those of the army, but the militiamen's weapons were generally much more expensively made, since they paid for them themselves and considered that only the best was good enough.

Each company had its own standard. Originally they each bore one of the colours of the States flag: orange, white or blue (light blue),

The entry of Maria de Medicis, into Amsterdam on 1 September 1638. Shown here is the triumphal arch on the Dam, with the procession of Maria de Medicis in front of it and the militia drawn up on either side.

The Doelheren of the Handbow Doelen in 1653, painted by Bartholomeus van der Helst. The man on the extreme left is Frans Banning Cocq, the captain of the *Nightwatch* (p.43).

but when the number of companies rose above three, standards were also made in a combination of those three colours or in different colours altogether. As far as their clothing was concerned, the militiamen were left complete freedom, though they did often wear scarves – officers invariably did so – and hang tassels on their spontoons or halberds in the colour or colours of the standard.

On these three prints by Jacob de Gheyn can be seen a musketeer with a light musket and one with a heavy musket, that had to be propped up on a long support with a forked end, and, in the centre, a *piekenier*.

The chain of the *Kloveniers* that was awarded annually to the best marksmen. Among the links of the chain has been incorporated the claw, the symbol of the *Kloveniers*.

The more the real functions of the militia declined, the more important became its ostentatious display. This finds expression in, among other things, the great militia pieces, like the *Nightwatch,* that the companies had painted. A good opportunity for the militia to appear in full regalia was the entry of some important personage into the city. In 1638 Amsterdam witnessed that of the Queen Mother of France, Maria de Medicis. At that precise moment she was in fact a monarch without a kingdom, for in consequence of long standing disagreements she had been sent into exile by her son Louis XIII and she was now wandering around Europe in search of the marks of honour commensurate with her former high rank. But Amsterdam was not a city to be small-minded: exiled or not, Maria de Medicis was given a reception worthy of a queen.

The organization of the entry involved no small degree of difficulty since it was not known until the last minute whether the queen would be arriving by land or by water. The authorities had decided that the entry was to be accompanied by "the whole of the militia in arms, by display and otherwise the highest honour". That meant that all along the route triumphal arches were erected, on each of which a sort of *tableau vivant* was performed. These preparations were made at white-hot speed, for the queen's impending arrival was announced half way through August and the actual entry took place on the first of September. The militiamen were drawn up all along the route, each company's position having been decided by the drawing of lots. Anyone not wishing to participate in this guard of honour had to pay a heavy fine and so the companies were present at virtually their full strength. But one spoilsport on the occasion was the weather: it rained. "But the splendour and the brilliant appearance of their garments, arms and ornaments were dampened and diminished by the rain that had fallen", so wrote the historian Gerard Schaep. And another spoilsport seems to have been the Queen herself: she evidently made no secret of the fact that she found the Amsterdammers but a rough pack of folk.

The Company of Kloveniers of Captain Jacob Symonsz. de Vries and Lieutenant Dirck de Graeff, group portrait painted in 1633 by Thomas de Keyser.

Armies were accompanied by sutlers and the militia too had female servants to wait on the militiamen in the Doelen. Sutlers mostly supplied beer, sausage and poultry and it may perhaps have been the poultry that inspired Rembrandt to incorporate the symbol of the *Kloveniers* into the *Nightwatch* in a clever way by adding the little girl with a chicken at her belt.

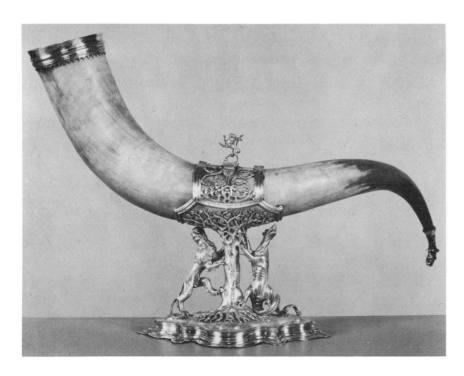

The drinking-horn of the *Kloveniers*, made in 1547.

The *Swijgh Utrecht* Tower, a drawing by Rembrandt. Rembrandt has omitted the *Doelen* building on the left.

"The *Doelen* Tower in Amsterdam on the water side, with its wooden bulwarks, as it was in the year 1607. Now altered into a fine street with houses that look out over the Binnenamstel".

Four years later, in 1642, Amsterdam again witnessed the entry of a queen: this time that of Henrietta Maria, Queen of England. Here again everything seemed much grander than it really was, for she had come to Holland to obtain help from the Republic for her husband Charles I, who at that moment was in serious difficulties with his parliament, and to pawn her crown jewels in exchange for arms. Admittedly this entry was not accompanied by so much display as that of Maria de Medicis, but it did nonetheless afford a fine opportunity for the militiamen to show off their accoutrements and their discipline. It was with the aim of recording their glory for longer than just a fleeting moment that the militiamen had been in the habit since as long ago as the sixteenth century of having their companies depicted in group portraits, which were then hung in the *Doelen.*

De DOELETOREN aen de waterzyde t'Amsterdam met zyne houte wallen, zoo als hy was in den Jaere 1607. tegenwoordig in een schoone straat met huyzen verandert, hebbende hun uytzicht op den Binnenamstel.

The commission

the guildhall of the militia companies – commissions for the militia pieces in the great hall – the *Nightwatch,* composition and militiamen – Rembrandt's personal circumstances

Since 1522 the Kloveniers had used the *Swijgh Utrecht* Tower as their guildhall, but it was not large and the more festive gatherings came to play an increasingly important role in the life of the militia, the more keenly the lack of space was felt. So it was decided to build an extension on an open site beside the tower. The new building was completed in or shortly before 1638. Caspar Barlaeus described it as "built anew most elegantly" and the new extension was indeed designed in the then ultra-modern classicist style, with flat pilasters with stone capitals and stone frames to the windows. The most important part of the extension was the great hall on the first floor, where the militiamen at last had plenty of room for their meetings. It measured about 18 metres by 9 and in one of the long walls there were six leaded windows wich looked out over the Amstel. The hall could only be reached by way of the old *Doelen* building. The entrance door was in one of its short walls and beside it stood a broad fireplace. There was a fireplace in the other short wall too, but it was a much narrower one.

The *Kloveniers* must already have decided while building was still in progress that the hall was to be decorated with group portraits

The *Swijgh Utrecht* Tower was built in the years 1481-2 as part of the fortifications of the city. The name *Swijgh Utrecht* (Keep Quiet, Utrecht) probably came into being at the same time as a result of a successful operation by the Amsterdam militia against an attack by troops from Utrecht on the town of Naarden. In 1522 the tower was assigned to the *Kloveniers* as their guildhall. A wooden footbridge was built to link it with the nearby practice-grounds.

The Kloveniersdoelen on the Amstel Side, a painting of 1775 by Jan Ekels (1724-81).

of their companies. Nor was there anything particularly startling about this idea as such, for the companies had already had portraits painted of themselves over the years, some of which hung in the old *Doelen* building. But now for the first time there was enough space to allow for all six companies of the *Kloveniersdoelen* to be painted at one and the same time. The exact course of events in relation to the commissions for these six militia pieces is not known to us, but it is certainly possible to imagine what the procedure was to some extent.

First of all the positions of the six paintings in the hall had to be determined: one on either side of the small fireplace, three on the long wall opposite the windows and one above the large fireplace. Above the small fireplace was to come a group portrait of the governors of the militia: the *Doelheren*.

It would also have been necessary to find out how many members of each company wanted to participate. Only those militiamen who were willing or able to pay for their own portraits were included in the paintings. For the officers that was no great problem; they always came of well-to-do families and could easily afford the expense of a portrait, but for the men it was another matter and mostly only about ten or fifteen of the ordinary militiamen in each company took part in a group portrait project.

Then it would have had to be worked out which position on the wall each of the six companies was to be assigned. And that was no easy task, for the positions were by no means of equal value. For example, the place to the right of the small fireplace was not nearly so good as that in the centre of the long wall. The militiamen probably solved this thorny problem in the same way as they determined their position in parades, by drawing lots.

After that it at last became possible to offer the commissions to the painters. Each group portrait was allotted to a different painter. That was the only way to ensure that the decoration would be finished within a reasonable time, for it took a considerable amount of time to paint a group portrait and the chosen painters – successful as they

Reconstruction of the arrangement of the paintings in the great hall of the *Kloveniersdoelen:* from left to right: Joachim von Sandrart, *The Company of Captain Cornelis Bicker,* 1638; Govert Flinck, *The Doelheren of the Kloveniers,* 1642; Govert Flinck, *The Company of Captain Albert Bas,* 1645; Rembrandt van Rijn, *The Company of Captain Frans Banning Cocq (The Nightwatch),* 1642; Nicolaes Eliasz., called Pickenoy, *The Company of Captain Jan Claesz. Vlooswijck,* 1642; Jacob Adriaensz. Backer, *The Company of Captain Cornelis de Graeff and Lieutenant Hendrick Lauwrensz.,* 1642; Bartholomeus van der Helst, *The Company of Captain Roelof Bicker,* 1639.

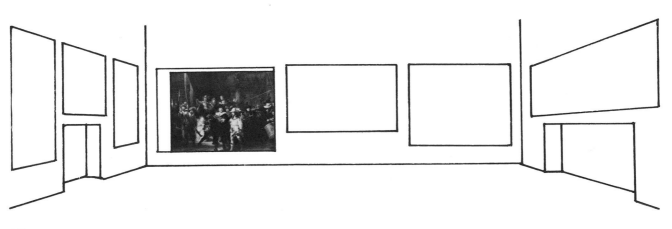

Rembrandt received 1,600 guilders, and perhaps even more, for his *Nightwatch.*

What was a guilder? The word comes from the coin value of 20 stuivers (five cent pieces) that was introduced under Charles V in 1521. It is a somewhat confusing word, since it indicates a gold coin (*gulden* = golden), but this was the guilder for only a relatively short time. The same name was later used for a silver coin which was struck for the first time in 1540. It had the same value. Although other types of coins from various areas were also to remain in circulation for a long while, Charles V's coin of the value of 20 stuivers, called simply guilder for short, became the monetary unit and was to remain such in the Netherlands up to the present day.
In 1642 the *Carolusgulden* passed out of use. For reasons of politics and the changes in the economy that they involved, there was a confusing variety of coins in circulation, which were struck in numerous Dutch towns. Ducats, rix-dollars, lion dollars, sovereigns, piastres, gold riders and florins from all over the place flooded the market. But the monetary unit remained, on paper, the guilder of 20 stuivers that no longer existed. Not until 1680 were new silver guilders made for the Republic of the United Netherlands.
It is difficult to make out exactly what such a guilder was worth in 1642, though one can get something of an idea by comparing the prices of those days with those of today.
On 5 January 1639 Rembrandt bought the house built in 1606 for 13,000 guilders; the restoration of the Rembrandthuis in 1974-5 cost around a million. We know too that for a portrait of the daughter of the rich merchant Diego d'Andrada Rembrandt was paid in 1654 an advance sum of 75 guilders, half the total fee agreed on. Well-known portrait painters today can easily ask around ten to fifteen thousand guilders for a portrait. A kilo of rye (the basis of the staple food of ordinary people at that time: rye bread), cost about a stuiver and a half then. In the middle of 1976 a kilo of rye floor cost around f 2.25 (i.e.) 45 stuivers, or thirty times as much as in 1642). A rough estimate thus shows that the guilder had about 25 times its present purchasing power then, so Rembrandt was certainly not badly paid for his *Nightwatch.*

These are a few of the very many coins that were in circulation in the Dutch Republic in Rembrandt's time. Top left, a Spanish piastre (= 8 reals), struck by Philip III in Mexico in 1606; next to it a double stuiver, West Friesland, 1615. Centre left, a lion dollar from Gelderland, 1628, and next to it, a Holland shilling of 1601; centre top, a Holland stuiver of 1614, below it, a Utrecht ducat of 1637, next to it a Zeeland doit of 1642. Bottom left, a Holland rix-dollar of 1644, centre, an Overijssel doit of 1628, right a florin (28 stuivers) of the town of Kampen of 1618.

A specie book is a handbook for the money market, in which coins that were more or less current were described.

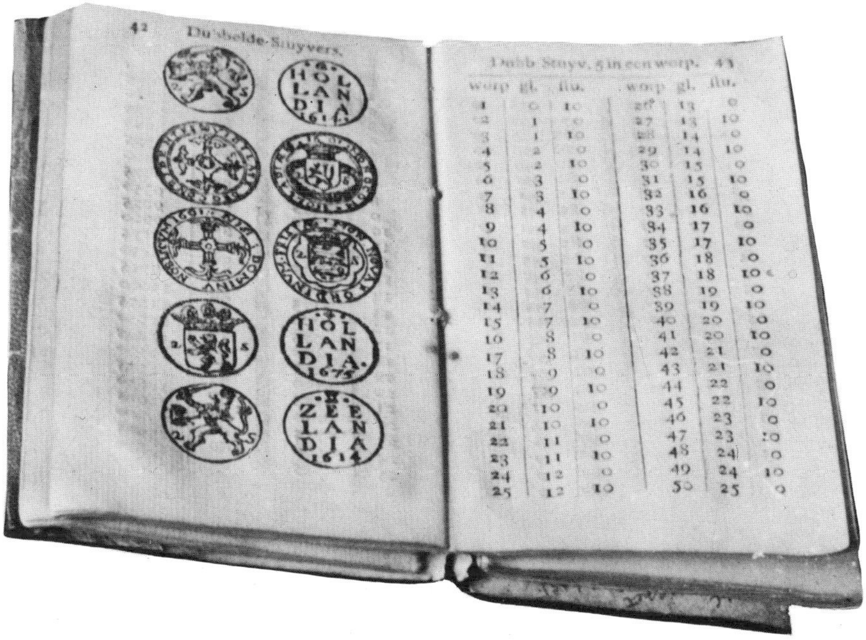

Aldernuttigst Vermeerderd en Verbeterd
SPECIEBOEK.
Bevattende in zig de Uitreekening van veele
GOUDE EN ZILVERE
SPECIEN;
Zeer dienstig voor die dagelyks veel Geld uitgeven en ontfangen.
Hier hebben wy by gevoegd de Afbeelding van eenige Goude Specien, benevens de Ducatons, RyksDaalders, Achtentwintigen, Schellingen en Dubbeltjes, benevens een Lyst op de Uitreekening der Brandewyn; als ook een Uitreekening op de Tonnen Turf, en het Verschil der Graan-Zakken en andere Maten, zeer dienstig voor die haar veel met de Graan-Negotie bemoeijen, als ook 't Verschil der Gewigten van 133 Koop-Steden.
TE AMSTERDAM,
By de ERFGEN. van de Wed. C. STICHTER, Boekverkopers op 't Rokkin, in de Oude Berg Calvarie.

Jacob Adriaensz. Backer was a Frisian. He was born in Harlingen in 1608 and, like Govert Flinck, he studied first under the Leeuwarden painter Lambert Jacobsz. After he had settled in Amsterdam in 1633, he conceived a great admiration for the work of Rembrandt. He remained a respected Amsterdam painter until his death on 27 August 1651.

all were – will undoubtedly still have had other work in hand as well. The six painters to whom the commissions were given were: Joachim von Sandrart, Govert Flinck, Rembrandt van Rijn, Nicolaes Eliasz. Pickenoy, Jacob Backer and Bartholomeus van der Helst. Govert Flinck was also to paint the chimney-piece portrait of the *Doelheren*. In accordance with the custom of the time, the painters will certainly have submitted a study for their paintings to the militiamen in the form of a drawing or a painted sketch on a small scale. In designing their compositions they would have to take account of the positions in the hall they had each been allotted and to the play of light there. But each of them also had to make his composition harmonize with that of the others and that was no simple proposition for Dutch painters at that time, for it only rarely happened in the Northern Netherlands that painters worked together on the decoration of a building. In other countries, such as Italy, France, or the Southern Netherlands, such a situation was a frequent occurence and painters managed to solve the problems involved with great skill, but in the Northern Netherlands – a country without a monarchy and thus with no large palaces, and with a Protestant church that preached simplicity above all else - large decorative schemes for palaces or churches were seldom or never undertaken. Thus that lack of experience will have been the reason why the co-operation in the

The Company of Captain Albert Bas and Lieutenant Lucas Conijn, 1645.

Govert Flinck was born in Germany (in Cleves on 25 January 1615), but he soon moved to the Netherlands, where he remained until his death (in Amsterdam on 2 February 1660). At the early age of sixteen he was already working as a pupil in the studio of the Leeuwarden painter Lambert Jacobsz., who enjoyed a great vogue at that time, but a year later he was in Amsterdam as one of the first pupils of the young Rembrandt, who had settled there for good in the autumn of 1631. He remained in Rembrandt's studio from 1632 until 1635, being very strongly influenced by him. After 1645 he adopted a more "modish" style than that of his teacher. He was a highly regarded and much sought after painter in Amsterdam, assisting, among other things, with the decoration of the new Town Hall (the Palace on the Dam).

The Doelheren of the Kloveniers in 1642: Albert Coenraetsz. Burgh, Jan Claesz. Vlooswijk, Pieter Reael and Jacob Willekens. The man without a hat is a servant.

The Company of Captain Cornelis de Graeff and Lieutenant Hendrick Lauwrensz., 1642 (p.50).

All the artists who painted militia pieces for the great hall of the *Kloveniersdoelen* included portraits of themselves among the heads of the militiamen. They are at the right- or left-hand edges of the painting and can easily be recognized by the fact that they are gazing straight at the spectator. Did Rembrandt, too, include a self-portrait in his militia piece? Is it his eye that is looking over the shoulder of one of the militiamen right at the back? Or is he the man whose face is half hidden by the outstretched arm of Sergeant Rombout Kemp?

The Nightwatch before the restoration of 1975-6.

Joachim von Sandrart was a German painter, who was born in Frankfurt-am-Main on 12 May 1606 and died in Nüremberg on 14 October 1688. He was a versatile and much-travelled man. He not only painted, but he also made drawings and etchings and wrote a large two-volume work on architecture, painting and sculpture. At the age of sixteen he went to Prague, where he became the pupil of Egidius Sadeler; in 1623 he was back in Frankfurt as the pupil of Sebastian Stosskopf and a few years later he was working in the studio of the Utrecht painter Gerard Honthorst. During a stay of several years in Amsterdam he received a commission from the *Kloveniers* for their new great hall.

decoration of the great hall in the Doelen does not appear to have been particularly successful. The painters allowed their own tastes and preferences to prevail over the idea of making the decoration look like a unified whole.

We do not know in which year the commissions for the group portraits in the hall of the *Kloveniersdoelen* were given or even whether they were all given at roughly the same time, but we do know that the paintings were by no means all finished at the same time. The first to be completed was that by Joachim von Sandrart in 1639, the last that by Govert Flinck in 1645.

Rembrandt van Rijn was given the commission to paint the company of Captain Frans Banning Cocq. The place assigned to him for the painting was on the left of the long wall. In addition to the officers, the captain, the lieutenant, the two sergeants and the ensign, thirteen other militiamen paid to be included. The drummer was also included, but he did not have to pay for his portrait himself, for his

The Company of Captain Jan Claesz. Vlooswijck and Lieutenant Gerrit Hudde, 1642 (p.55).

The Company of Captain Cornelis Bicker and Lieutenant Frederick van Banchem, 1638. In the foreground is a bust of Maria de Medicis and on the piece of paper is a poem by Vondel that states that the group portrait was painted on the occasion of her visit to Amsterdam in 1638.

function was not an honorary one like those of the militiamen. He was in the service of the militia and was generally paid for his work. Of these nineteen portraits only seventeen are still to be seen on the painting, since in the 18th century a strip containing two portraits was cut off the painting on the left side. Surviving documents reveal that each of the militiamen portrayed by Rembrandt paid around a hundred guilders for his portrait – some slightly more, others slightly less, according to the place they occupied in the painting. A hundred guilders was a normal fee in those days for inclusion in a militia piece. In the documents it is also stated that sixteen militiamen paid their hundred guilders but in fact eighteen were portrayed in the painting. The captain and the lieutenant may well have made their payments separately and they probably also came to more than a hundred guilders. Their positions as the two main figures in Rembrandt's painting would certainly have justified such an exceptional fee. For Rembrandt each new commission was a challenge, a challenge to depict precisely that action, that moment in his painting that would give it tension and make it arresting. For him that tension, that arresting moment was the most important element in a painting, whether it was a portrait, a group portrait or a Biblical scene.

Thus when he received the commission to paint a group portrait of

Nicolaes Eliasz., called Pickenoy, was an Amsterdammer and the oldest of the six painters who were commissioned to decorate the great hall of the *Kloveniersdoelen*. He was born in Amsterdam in 1590 or 1591 and died there between 1654 and 1656. He too was a well-known portrait painter and Bartholomeus van der Helst was probably a pupil of him. Nicholas Eliasz. lived next-door to Rembrandt in Sint Anthonies Breestraat.

The *Nightwatch* after the restoration
of 1975-6.

56

Bartholomeus van der Helst was born in Haarlem in 1613. He came to Amsterdam as a young portrait painter in training, probably finding a teacher in Eliasz. He became a celebrated painter of portraits, his work being influenced by the styles of both his former fellow-townsman Frans Hals and Rembrandt. He died in Amsterdam and was buried there on 16 December 1670.

a militia company, his first thought must have been: what shall I show happening in that painting, what action shall I put into it? And as a result, instead of making of the commission a skilfully composed collection of portraits, he chose an event for it: Captain Banning Cocq is giving Lieutenant Van Ruytenburch the command to have the militia company march off. That gave Rembrandt an opportunity to involve each of the people portrayed in the painting in the action. The sergeant on the far right is passing the order on and motioning a militiaman into position. The other sergeant is shown on the far left. The men are busily occupied with their weapons: muskets are being loaded and fired and at the back the *piekeniers* are manoeuvring with their pikes. As for the objects such as old weapons, old helmets and the guild's cup, which the militiamen wanted to be included as symbols of their glorious past, Rembrandt was too much of a history painter just to put them in without giving them any function. So he showed the old helmets being worn and the old weapons being used and placed the cup in the hand of the little girl in yellow. He took great pains, too, to imbue the events in his militia piece with a definite meaning. In other militia pieces the arms of the officers are obvious distinguishing marks to show who is who, but in Rembrandt's painting that is not necessary. Even without the distinguishing marks the ranks are perfectly clear: the captain is giving the order, the lieutenant is receiving it, the one sergeant is passing it on and although the other sergeant is not quite so active, he still occupies a striking place. It is also immediately apparent that we have to do with the *Kloveniers,* the arquebusiers, here, the guild that used fire-arms from

the time of its foundation. The handling of the musket is an important part of the action in the painting: we see it being loaded by the man in red and fired behind the back of the captain, and the remaining powder being blown away by the man to the right of the lieutenant. The other weapons of a militia company are also clearly shown, the round shields of the *rondassiers* on the left and the pikes of the *piekeniers* at the back. Rembrandt has further found a highly inventive way of representing the fact that the symbol of the *Kloveniers* is a claw: on the belt of the little girl in yellow a chicken is hanging in such a way that its claws in particular are clearly visible. Such a chicken is also often to be seen in depictions of sutlers, along with other comestibles and, just as in the case of the little girl, a purse. Thus Rembrandt has actually made the little girl into a miniature sutler, as well as a sort of mascot, since she also carries a pistol at her belt.

The small boys in the painting are powder boys, welcome assistants in the complicated process of preparing muskets for firing. The boy behind the captain is wearing oak leaves round his helmet. For the militiamen oak leaves were the symbol of the power of the citizenry and claws and oak leaves were the motifs on the silver chain that the winner of the annual shooting competition might hold for a year as a sort of trophy. Rembrandt also used the figures of children in his painting for the sake of the composition, in order to create some space in the picture, just as the dog serves to separate the two main figures from the rest of the company.

Rembrandt was very well aware that his picture would be hung on the left of the long wall in the *Kloveniersdoelen* and that a direct

On the shield on the gate in the *Nightwatch* can be read the following names:
Frans Banning Cocq
lord of Purmerlant and Ilpendam
Captain
Willem van Ruytenburch van
Vlaerdingen
lord of Vlaerdingen lieutenant
Jan Visscher Cornelisen ensign
Rombout Kemp Sergeant
Reinier Engelen Sergeant
Barent Harmansen
Jan Adriaensen Keijser
Elbert Willemsen
Jan Clasen Leijdeckers
Jan Ockersen
Jan Pietersen bronchorst
Harman Iacobsen wormskerck
Jacob Dircksen de Roy
Jan van der heede
Walich Schellingwou
Jan brugman
Claes van Gruysbergen
Paulus Schoonhoven

The Company of Captain Roelof Bicker and Lieutenant Jan Michielsz. Blaeuw, 1639.

view of the left-hand side of the painting would be impeded by the projecting fireplace on the short wall. He thus also took account of this in his composition, by placing the sergeant on the left not on the edge of the painting, but somewhat to the right, with three more figures to the left of and slightly behind him. That compositional effect can no longer be seen, since the painting has been cut down on the left. A further consequence of this way of composing the picture was that the two main figures, the captain and the lieutenant, stand not in the centre, but slightly to the right of it, so that the feeling of movement in the painting is made even stronger.

The names of the militiamen portrayed by Rembrandt are all known – they are, after all, inscribed on the shield that hangs on the gateway – but in only a few instances do we know which name belongs to which person. The militiamen in the *Nightwatch* were those of District II,

The Officers of St. George's or the Crossbow Doelen, Haarlem, painted by Frans Hals in 1616.

i.e. the Damrak ("the Water") and Nieuwendijk. Most of them were merchants, drapers in the main, for Nieuwendijk had been the centre of the cloth trade since the sixteenth century.

Captain Frans Banning Cocq (1605-55) is an example of how in the sixteenth and seventeenth centuries a family could acquire great wealth and prestige in one generation. His father had come to Amsterdam from Bremen without a penny to his name. There he was taken in by an apothecary and later on he himself opened an apothecary's shop and married a daughter of a prominent Amsterdam family of the name of Benning or Banning. Their son Frans acquired the surnames of both his father and mother. He studied law, taking a doctorate in the subject. He married a daughter of the Amsterdam burgomaster Overlander and after the death of his father-in-law in 1630 he became Lord of Purmerend and Ilpendam.

One sometimes finds the term "corporalship" used in connection with militia pieces (like the *Nightwatch*), but this is incorrect. A corporalship was a section of a militia company, usually consisting of about thirty men. Admittedly the number of militiamen generally to be seen on the paintings more or less tallies with the complement of a corporalship, but all the officers of the company as a whole are always shown as well, while a corporalship was commanded by only one officer of higher or lower rank. Thus what we see on such a militia piece is a representation of a whole company. Moreover only those who helped to pay for the picture might appear in it. As far as that is concerned, the *Nightwatch* with its sixteen (originally eighteen) men may even be called small as a total representation. The group portraits of the Haarlem militia (painted by Frans Hals and others) show only the officers of the whole militia together. They comprised three captains, three lieutenants and three ensigns. The sergeants were not generally included, but places were found for the colonel, who was above all the other officers, and the master-at-arms, who looked after the financial affairs.

In 1712 there came up at for sale in Amsterdam a painting that was described as follows in the sale catalogue: "The *Doelen* piece, in which appears Captain Benning Kok with his Militia, painted in detail by Gerard Lundens, the best work by him known". The measurements of the painting are not given in the catalogue, but it has been identified with a copy of the *Nightwatch* that has been on loan to the Rijksmuseum since 1958 from the National Gallery in London and on these grounds it has been taken that the painter of this copy must be Gerrit Lundens (1622- after 1683). At present, however, people are not quite so certain of this any more, since Gerrits Lundens' style of painting is not really much like that of the copy. The peculiar interest of this copy is that it probably shows the original composition of the *Nightwatch*, before it was cut down on all sides, and especially on the left, presumably in 1715. There also exist a number of other copies of the *Nightwatch* that show it at its original size: a watercolour drawing in the family album of Captain Frans Banning Cocq, done between 1642 and 1655, a drawing of 1762 by Hendrik Pothoven, a watercolour drawing of 1779 by Jacob Cats and an engraving of 1797 by L.A. Claessens. However, these copies need not all have been done from the original painting. It is much more likely that they were copied from each other or that they go back to a small painted copy of the *Nightwatch*. Banning Cocq probably had such a copy in his possession. At all events there is one to be found in the inventory of his heirs. It quite often happened that the main figure on a large painting of this sort, that was meant for a public building, had a small copy painted to hang up at home.

thus acquiring a house, *Ilpenstein,* at Ilpendam and a fine town house, *The Dolphin,* on the Singel in Amsterdam. He rapidly made a career for himself in the city government: as early as 1632 he was a member of the matrimonial affairs board, he became an alderman and from 1650 to 1652 and again in 1653 he was burgomaster of Amsterdam. In 1635 he became lieutenant of District I in the *Kloveniers* militia and between 1639 and 1642 captain of District II. He further became a regent or *Doelheer* of an older and thus more prestigious guild, that of the Handbow Archers. Frans Banning Cocq was proud of his wife's family and his own career. He collected drawings of everything relating to them in a two-volume family album and in that book there was also a drawing of the *Nightwatch.*

Lieutenant Willem van Ruytenburch (1600-52) was entitled to style himself Lord of Vlaardingen, since he had bought the manor of Vlaardingen. He too married a wife from a notable Amsterdam family. His political career began in 1639 with his election to the council and in 1641 he became an alderman. He likewise owned a fine house in Amsterdam, one on Oude Zijds Achterburgwal, which his father had bought in 1606.

Ensign Jan Visscher Cornelissen was unmarried, handsome and strong, as it behoved an ensign to be, although they were not always so owing to a lack of suitable candidates. Little more is known about him, except that he died, still unmarried, in 1650.

The sergeant on the right was Rombout Kemp, a draper of Nieuwendijk. In 1646 he became the lieutenant of the company of District II in Van Ruytenburch's stead. He was also regent of the Nieuwe Zijds Outdoor Relief House. He died in 1654.

The sergeant on the left, Reynier Engelen, was also a draper. He was born in 1591 or 1592, so at the time the *Nightwatch* was painted he was already 51 years old. He died in 1651.

Of the others only the identity of the *piekenier* with the tall plumed hat on the right is known. He was Jacob Dircksen de Roy.

The setting of the action of the painting has been the subject of a great deal of discussion. It is clearly not the entrance to the *Kloveniersdoelen,* for that was much more modest in its dimensions. It has also been suggested that the Palace on the Dam served as a model, or

Three well-known copies after Rembrandt's *Nightwatch* are reproduced on p. 62.

Above:
Copy of the *Nightwatch,* attributed to Gerrit Lundens (see also p.90).

Centre:
Copy of the copy of the *Nightwatch* attributed to Lundens, a watercolour of 1779 by Jacob Cats.

Below:
Engraving after the *Nightwatch* by L.A. Claessens, 1797.

Drawings of c. 1650 from the family album of Frans Banning Cocq.
The *Nightwatch:* "the painting in the Great Hall of the *Kloveniers Doelen"* (left).
The house *Ilpenstein* at Ilpendam, the manor of Frans Banning Cocq from 1630 on (right).

The Register of Burials of the Oude Kerk in Amsterdam with the record of Saskia's burial on 19 June 1642.

Two Women and a Child by the Door of a House, a drawing by Rembrandt of around 1635.

one of the city gates of Amsterdam, or perhaps one of the triumphal arches put up for the entry of Maria de Medicis or even the permanent set of the new Amsterdam theatre that was opened in 1639. However, none of these models has precisely the same construction as that used by Rembrandt in his painting, which was in all probability an invention of his own, perhaps inspired by such monumental gateways as were to be seen in Amsterdam.

There is even less reason to suppose that Rembrandt was intending to depict an actual event. The daily turn-out of the watch was a scene well known to every Amsterdammer and certainly to Rembrandt, who lived almost next-door to the *Kloveniersdoelen* at one stage. But on such occasions neither the two commanding officers nor the drummer was present. Nor did the militiamen appear in their full regalia at such times, though that was the case when they turned out to put in an appearance at an entry. On the basis of this last fact, it has been suggested that Rembrandt was intending to depict the company's attendance at the entry of Maria de Medicis in 1638, but that is ruled out by the fact that Banning Cocq had not yet become the captain of the company of District II by then. The composition is probably a situation "stage-managed" by Rembrandt himself, for which he drew on his memories of the militia turning out, but in which he also realized his idea of making a meaningful event of it.

In the sixteen-thirties and forties Rembrandt was as successful as any artist could wish to be, but in his private life the situation was not so rosy. Documents record the death of a little son, Rumbartus, in 1636 two months after his birth, of a little daughter, Cornelia, in 1638 shortly after her birth, and of another Cornelia in 1640. In September 1641 Titus was born and he did manage to survive. Drawings of those years show an ailing Saskia in bed or dozing in a chair. She was not yet thirty, but she looks old and tired. She died on 14 June 1642, being buried in the Oude Kerk on 19 June. Around 1643 a young widow, Geertge Dircks, came into Rembrandt's household to look after Titus. She came from Ransdorp, a village near Amsterdam. She seems to have been on the best possible terms with her employer at first, but around 1649 a change took place and a series of sordid law-suits put an end to the relationship. Rembrandt was ordered to pay her 200 guilders a year alimony, but shortly afterwards, on his initiative and probably on somewhat flimsy grounds, she was ordered to be confined for twelve years in a house of correction at Gouda. Fortunately some friends of hers managed to get her released after five years. She probably died shortly afterwards.

The reason for all this wrangling was probably the arrival in Rembrandt's house of a new servant, Hendrickje Stoffels. She eventually came to fulfil the role of a wife in every respect and she is

Self portrait of Rembrandt and a
portrait of Saskia of 1640 and 1641,
paintings that may well once have
been companion pieces. The portrait
of Rembrandt himself was probably
not rounded off at the top untill the
18th century.

even referred to as Rembrandt's wife *(huysvrou)* in an official document, although the union was never legally sanctioned.

Rembrandt's career continued to prosper through those years of personal troubles. He did paintings on commission, and etchings as well, but he also produced numerous etchings and paintings of his own invention, which were then sold to interested customers either by himself or through an art-dealer. In fact he never became the forgotten painter who is presented with so much relish in so many books. Even after his bankruptcy in 1656 and his removal in 1660 to a smaller house in a more modest neighbourhood, he was still a painter to reckon with. In 1661 he painted his *Claudius Civilis* as a decoration for the new Town Hall. Admittedly, the painting was never put in the place it was intended for, but whether that was really because the city council dit not want to accept it is open to question. Also in 1661 he painted a *Homer* and an *Alexander the Great* for the Italian nobleman Antonio Ruffo, who further bought 189 etchings from him. In 1662 he painted the *Syndics,* the controllers of the Drapers' Guild, and when Cosimo de' Medici, the later Grand Duke of Tuscany paid a visit to Amsterdam in 1667, a call at Rembrandt's studio was an indispensable item on the programme.

Portrait of an unknown married couple depicted as two old Testament figures, painted by Rembrandt around 1665. This picture is usually known as *The Jewish Bride,* a title that was not given to it until 19th century.

Amsterdam in the Golden Age

reading and listening – glimpses of cultural, intellectual and spiritual life –
the everyday atmosphere

The intellectual climate of Rembrandt's Amsterdam in the first half of the seventeenth century was almost as explosive as the economic. With the enormous growth in its population, which had trebled in fifty years or so, the city had been plunged into a maelstrom of new ideas. Literature and art, architecture, religion and thought, medicine and the exact sciences flourished as never before and as much as they had done anywhere else in the previous centuries, centuries in which Antwerp had set the tone much more than Amsterdam, which was then little more than a village. Bled dry by the Inquisition, the persecuted and the non-conformists of Antwerp had found their way to the rapidly growing city on the Amstel which promised them freedom, albeit a freedom only of tolerance and a freedom of which the economic profit to be made out of it was by no means the least important foundation. The Amsterdam authorities continued to give their formal support to the only recognized religion, Calvinism, and the only recognized economic system, that of the guilds, but in both instances a bit of compromise here and there did not come amiss, for, after all, those who turned a blind eye to dissenting opinions or divergent trading methods could do very nicely out of it materially speaking, as long as those views and methods were not propagated or practised too openly.

All this had in a short time a much more explosive character than it had had, earlier on, in neighbouring countries. The stabilization of the Dutch language is perhaps the most eloquent example of this. It happened only at a relatively late date, in the last quarter of the sixteenth and first half of the seventeenth century and, as mostly happened elsewhere too, it found its definitive form in literary landmarks (Hooft, Bredero, Cats, Vondel) and in the official translation of the Bible, the *Statenbijbel,* published in 1637.

The process had been much the same elsewhere, although it had occurred a good deal earlier in many cases, and the literature and the Bible in the vernacular had throughout Europe, *i.e.* the world of those days, been the basis on which ordinary people could acquire their knowledge. Italy laid the foundations of her language with the works of Dante, Petrarch and Boccaccio as early as the first half of the fourteenth century, the period of the early Renaissance which was to have such a powerful influence on the whole world in

Pieter Cornelisz. Hooft (1581-1647), who came from a wealthy and distinguished background and received a classical education, devoted himself mainly to tragedy and poetry. In his young days it was primarily to the girls of Amsterdam that he dedicated his, often erotic, verses. The Renaissance had a very deep influence on him and it is because of that that many people find his literary work somewhat inaccessible nowadays. All the same, at the beginning of the 17th century he was one of the most important creators of the "new" Dutch language.

succeeding centuries. In France the language had been put on a sound footing by the fifteenth-century writers François Villon and Charles d'Orléans, by the Renaissance poets of the sixteenth century and by the Burgundian rhetoricians, who, among other things, served as a model for Netherlandish rhetoricians. In England the language took shape under the strong influence of Henry VIII (1491-1547), so often dismissed in a high-handed manner on account of his private life, in figures like Cranmer (translator of the Bible) and Sir Thomas Elyot (poet) and reached a peak of brilliance in Shakespeare and the Authorized Version of the Bible (1611). In Germany, which almost merged with the Netherlands without any very clear dividing-line, Luther's translation of the Bible (1522-34) was an event which reached far beyond that country's frontiers, while in Spain the literary golden age, the sixteenth century, with its centres in Salamanca and Seville was almost over by the time of the war with the Netherlands (1568-1648).

All this had penetrated to the Northern Netherlands thanks to the spread of the art, invented around 1450, of setting and printing books, pamphlets and news-sheets with movable type, but not until after the general Reformation, around the end of the sixteenth century, did it come to great fruition there.

Language is a weapon. Latin, once the language of clergy and

The Amsterdam Roadstead, a painting by Abraham Storck. In the foreground a pinnace of the West India Company.

The *Paalhuis* near the New Bridge, where the boatmen had to pay their harbour dues and where they could also hand in letters addressed to people in the city (p. 69).

scholars, was, especially in the Middle Ages, an unbridgeable chasm between the learned and the unlearned classes. The latter could be and were driven into the corner of servitude and obedience, on pain of eternal punishment in the fires of hell, by the magic of the learned Latinists, who also had their rulers in their power because of it. During the Renaissance in the fifteenth and sixteenth centuries the realization dawned that the unlearned also wanted to acquire knowledge. And that knowledge was also at a given moment to lead to the Reformation, the great popular spiritual revolt against the abuses and exploitation whereby the church and the rulers bolstered up by it tyrannized the people. So it was that the Netherlands rose in revolt against the domination from afar of the Spanish monarchy in a war of eighty years' duration, which, though difficult at first, quite soon began to promise the hope of freedom and independent sovereignty and was eventually to fall out to the advantage of the rebels.

Eighty years? In reality, the outcome was already decided shortly after the famous battle of Nieuwpoort in 1600 and with the conclusion of the Twelve Years' Truce in 1609 the Republic of the United Netherlands was recognized as an independent state. It had in fact already been acting as such in the preceding decades, recognized or not, and although it was to suffer a few more hard knocks in the

Gerardus Vossius (1577-1649), was a famous philologist and historian, who wrote a great number of works on the history of Greek and Latin. He was Professor of Rhetoric and Greek at Leiden University and from 1631 onward taught history at the *Athenaeum Illustre* in Amsterdam.

Jacob Cats (1577-1660) was, in the
first place, a statesman, but he made
such a great name for himself as, above
all, a popular poet, that he even came
to be called "Father Cats". In the
innumerable prose writings, poems,
verses, sayings and anecdotes he wrote,
the average Dutch burgher could
recognize himself and his own
opinions.

Southern provinces of Brabant and Limburg after the resumption
of hostilities, the clock could never be set back again. Rembrandt
had scarcely settled in Amsterdam for good when the Republic
became one of the most powerful states in Europe, concluding
alliances with France and Sweden. Its own unique character had
been formed and could no longer be denied, a character based on
an economy that, while certainly not democratic, was as solid as a rock.
It is difficult to define the character of a people and even more so in
the case of a city and country to which so many fugitives from
oppression had brought clear contributions of their own: citizens
of Antwerp with their immensely rich language, German, Polish
and Hungarian free-thinkers of various persuasions, Portuguese
Jews with their profound reverence for learning. In this melting-pot
they came to terms with one another not only in learned disputes,
in theological controversy and hair-splitting, in literary rivalry, in
a quite unique form of painting and in a strong, unassuming architecture, but also in the seriousness of a deep faith, the gaiety of the
fair, the fantasy of the theatre and the earthiness of farce and low
comedy. And above all this there was a curious kind of simplicity
of life, which led the merchants for all their great wealth to live in
quite unpretentious houses, unlike their colleagues in other countries.
Money was there to make money, not to spend on luxury. This was
that thriftiness that later made the adjective Dutch in English a

byword for everything that appeared stingy and narrow-minded. And then there was that peculiar Dutch industriousness that caused a French writer of that time to remark on one occasion that a Dutch workman did more work in one day than a Frenchman did in a week. But there are things missing from this summary that are at least as important in determining the character of a people as those that appear in it. Apart from Spinoza, Holland had no philosopher of significance and the one it did have was vilified and denounced as a heretic. Apart from the De Keysers and Quellijn it had scarcely any sculptors, so it was, and still is for the most part today, a country without statues and monuments. After the death of Sweelinck in 1621, although *collegia musica* continued to make music and church organists gave public concerts, no more composers of international standing appeared on the scene, charming though Constantijn Huygens' *Pathodia* and Heiman Dullaerts' songs undoubtedly are. Reading and listening: that was the most important thing after all. Political events and sensational happenings appeared in the weekly

The Regents of the Nieuwe Zijds Huiszittenhuis, the Amsterdam Poor-house, a painting by Jacob Adriaensz. Backer. One of the regents is Rombout Kemp, who appears as a sergeant in the *Nightwatch,* but exactly which one he is is not known.

Fancy-dress parties were one of the pleasures of the 17th century. This young woman who, dressed as a peasant girl, is reading out a poem, was painted by Gerard ter Borch.

Constantijn Huygens (1596-1687) was a man of many parts. In the first place he was a diplomat (secretary to the Stadholder and the council of State) and he belonged to the Dutch aristocracy; alongside this he was a highly productive poet and composer who could identify himself completely with the feelings of the "common people". In intervals of his many diplomatic journeys and cares he applied himself to classical and modern languages, to theology and philosophy and he associated equally with the literary circle around P.C. Hooft and the academic circles around John Donne and René Descartes. His literary work in Dutch is sometimes very difficult (*Ship Talk* and the lyrical *Cornflowers* are among his most famous works), but sometimes it is even imbued with a coarse realism, as in the case of his farce *Trijntje Cornelis,* which was put on again not so long ago. As a composer he must have written hundreds of works, but virtually all of them have been lost. A single song cycle, *Pathodia sacra et profana* of 1647, has been preserved and was recently reprinted (1975).

At the end of the 1620's Huygens was one of the first people to "discover" the then still young painter, Rembrandt, and to prophesy a great future for him.

news-sheets brought out by the couranteers. They included foreign news too and that was of the greatest importance, since the Dutch drew most of their wealth from abroad. People read the news-sheets for themselves, read them out to others and passed on their contents by word of mouth, and the events in them were held up to ridicule or lauded to the skies in political and religious lampoons, which might or might not be in (halting) verse.

There was, indeed, an unstoppable impulse to write poetry, from doggerel to literature. It was often done in the context of a society. In Amsterdam there were two clubs, The Eglantine and The White Lavender, which were still always referred to as Chambers of Rhetoric, even though the rhetoric of the sixteenth century had long since become silted up in dead formal language. These clubs comprised groups of generally well-to-do amateurs who, in contrast to the painters, practised their art purely for the love of it. And they did nonetheless produce highwater marks in Dutch literature, which present-day Dutchmen scarcely know about, since the compilers of school textbooks seem to select the most boring examples with a well-nigh uncanny accuracy.

In the limited space available here it is not possible to give even a survey, let alone an appraisal of the influence these amateurs had on the language. But it is probably characteristic of this country that to the average Dutchman of today their best-known work is generally the weighty religious poetry, while all of them, from high to low, from famous to forgotten, did nonetheless often apply themselves to an enchantingly light lyricism. The best example of this is probably Bredero (1585-1618), actually the only playwright whose pieces, *De Spaanse Brabander* and *Moortje,* are still performable today, notwithstanding the age-long tradition of Vondel's *Gysbrecht van Aemstel,* which still lingers on. Bredero's short, intense life hurtled to and from between church and tavern and, as he said:

> *Wat dat de wereld is*
> *Dat weet ik al te wis*
> *(God betert) door 't verzoeken:*
> *Want ik heb daar verkeerd*
> *En meer van haar geleerd*
> *Als van de beste boeken.*

An aerial photograph of the part of Amsterdam where Rembrandt lived for much of his life. On the right is the Jodenbreestraat where the Rembrandthuis stands, on the left the Amstel with a view of the Doelen Hotel at the corner of the Kloveniersburgwal.

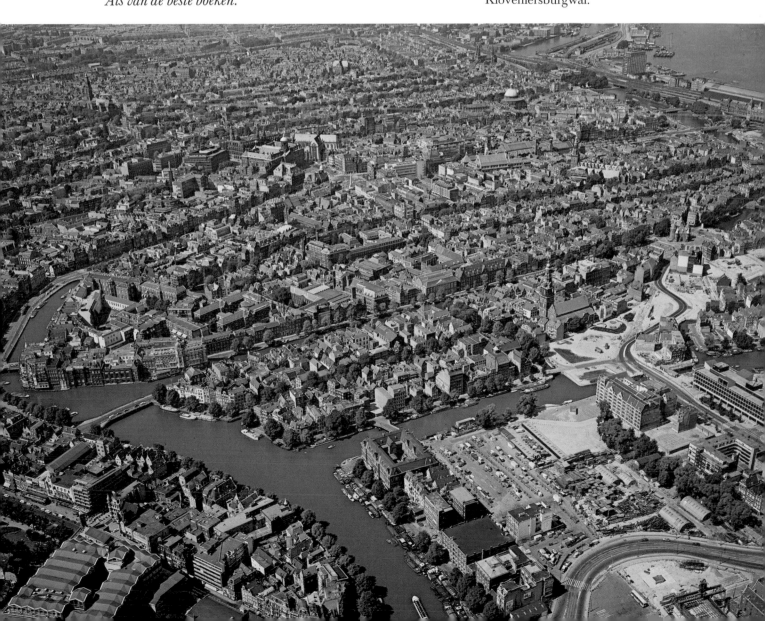

The First Dutch Academy, founded by Samuel Coster in 1617, which was in fact the first theatre in Amsterdam. It was closed down again in 1622.

DE EERSTE SCHOUWBURG TE AMSTERDAM,
COSTERS NEDERDUITSCHE ACADEMIE

Heiman Dullaert (1636-1684) was a painter, a pupil of Rembrandt (see bottom right), composer and, above all, a poet. He was "rediscovered" at the beginning of this century by Albert Verwey. Writing about good sonnets Verwey says of him: "Dullaert is the only one who comes into consideration here. Moreover, he is new. He has a deep, sweet tone that pierces senses and soul, that has a different, easily distinguishable gradation in each sonnet and that is at once enjoyable and painful. In the good sonnets (among which I do not include all of them) this tone moves with a pure dignity and quiet grace that has no need to bow before Hooft's heavier rhythm, ascending on high through the quatrains to turn back and as it were into itself in alarm and sudden disquiet. It is because he makes the sonnet into the form of this modesty that steps outside itself for a moment and then flees back again that Dullaert is such an exceptional original among the Dutch sonneteers". (A. Verwey, *Proza,* Vol. V, 1912).

De houding, koloryt, en Schaduwen, en licht,
Verschieten, en wat meer 't penceel heeft aen te merken,
Vertoonde ons DULLAERT in zyn uitgelezen werken.
De zelve deugt bezielt zyn zuiver maet gedicht.
Dat vry van Zwelling, vry van lasse en laege toonen,
Hem ons verbeelt als een van Febus waerdste zoonen.
D. VAN HOOGSTRATEN.

Joost van den Vondel (1587-1679) was already dubbed the "Prince among our poets" in his lifetime. He came of a Mennonite family that had fled to Amsterdam from Cologne and as a budding poet he became a member of the Chamber of Rhetoric, The White Lavender. He wrote a great many plays in verse, one of which, his *Gysbrecht van Aemstel*, written in 1637 for the opening of Amsterdam's new theatre, is still regularly performed today. Around 1640 he became a Catholic, but this never stood in the way of his acquiring literary commissions. His other plays are scarcely performable any more, but his short lyrics still retain their fascination.

Ground plan of the Amsterdam theatre designed by Jacob van Campen and built in 1637.

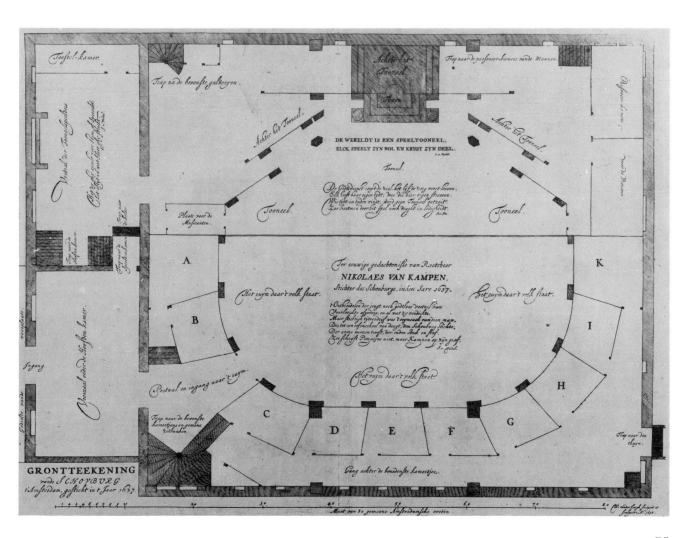

Protestantism was the generally recognized religion of Amsterdam in the 17th century. A Protestant church was sober in aspect and it differed in some respects from the Protestant churches of today. Three of those differences can bee seen in this painting by Emanuel de Witte: there were scarcely any pews in the church; it was open every day as a refuge from bad weather, so that anyone could go in, men with their hats on and even dogs; and people were still buried there, witness the open grave in the foreground. De Witte has here painted a generalized Protestant church rather than a particular one. His picture contains elements of both the Old and New Churches in Amsterdam.

Gerbrand Adriaensz. Bredero (1585-1618). At an early age he became a member of the Chamber of Rhetoric, The Eglantine, where he got to know Samuel Coster and P.C. Hooft, among others. During his short life he wrote a number of plays, popular poems, love songs and sonnets.

(What the world is, that I know all too well [God knows] from asking: for I have courted it and learned more from it than from the best books).

It is pointless to ask who was the "greatest" among them: the elegant, learned Hooft, the deeply religious, puzzleheaded, smooth-tongued Vondel, the moralizing Cats, who was also not averse to describing sensual pleasure, the scholarly Constantijn Huygens, who put farces and comedies full of *double entendres* on the stage, or Rembrandt's pupil Heiman Dullaert, too long forgotten, but perhaps the purest and simplest of them all in tone. Together they shaped the literary language and they also in many instances give a splendid picture of the language spoken in the streets by ordinary Amsterdammers. As far as this last in concerned, we can now only guess what it sounded like, but it was assuredly already as varied and witty then as the language of Amsterdam still is today.

In addition to The Eglantine and The White Lavender there was also the First Dutch Academy of the physician Samuel Coster, the son of a carpenter. This academy, which was in being from 1617 to

From the end of the 16th century Jews were allowed to profess their religion openly in Amsterdam. This painting of the interior of the Synagogue of the Portuguese Jews in Amsterdam is by Emanuel de Witte. In the foreground is the area reserved for Jewish women and non-Jews, behind the railing Jewish men at prayer.

A Musical Party, a painting by Johan Verkolje. At small musical parties held at home the instrumentalists mostly improvised, rather than playing from written music, though the voice part was set down in notation.

1622, represented a shortlived attempt to "help the people to enjoy the sciences in the vernacular". It was a sort of extension college, where "stone-masons, carpenters and bricklayers" took courses in mathematics, navigation and even Hebrew, and it met that hunger for knowledge in a way that was soon rendered impossible by the rigid Calvinist ministers, for that highly vaunted Amsterdam freedom was not yet as great as all that. Official learning fell back on the Latinist scholars who, under Vossius and Barlaeus, were united in the *Athenaeum Illustre* (now the University), which was founded in 1632. But the spirit of popular scientists like Simon Stevin, who, with both feet firmly on the ground, had maintained that "Miracle is no miracle" and had *en passant* relegated the notion of perpetual motion to the realm of fable, still continued to exist. And no wonder among a people who had reclaimed land from the sea and lakes of brackish water and to whom, with their ever more complicated seafaring, a knowledge of mathematics, geography and navigation was as necessary as their daily bread. Students of nature like Stevin, Beeckman, Snellius and Leeghwater had at least as much influence on the national character in Rembrandt's time as did the writers.

In studying life in Holland in the first half of the seventeenth century,

Bredero's tragi-comedy *Lucelle* was based on a French play by Le Jars. It was highly successful and was published in book form in 1622. That it remained in the repertoire for years is proved by this painting by Jan Miense Molenaer, which was done in 1636 and which shows the final scene in which Lucelle declares her love.

An Actor, perhaps a member of one of the English theatrical troupes that made regular visits to Amsterdam. A drawing by Rembrandt of around 1635.

An etching by Rembrandt that probably shows a pall-mall alley. Pall-mall was a popular ball game in the 17th century. It was played indoors by small groups.

one may succumb to the temptation of thinking about it in terms of our own time. Permeated as we are, whether consciously or unconsiously, with modern psychological and sociological ideas, we are readily inclined to wonder whether there can have been anyone in the seventeenth century who was not driven half out of his mind by guilt complexes. After all Calvinism, the established religion, taught the absolute power of God and His predestination of every human life in the hereafter for all eternity. It hammered away at one thing only: the question of sin and mercy, original sin in which state man was born and love, mercy, which one might perhaps be able to obtain in the hereafter – albeit only God would decide – as the result of a strictly austere and deeply devout life here on earth – and all that without the temporary earthly comfort of confession and indulgence, whereby the Catholic Church had offered a measure of certainty as to the number of years or centuries a poor wretch would have to spend in purgatory or hell after his life of drudgery on earth. This all added up, of course, to a belief in a God Who was more inscrutable and unpredictable and probably much more vindictive. But the Amsterdam merchants, who on Sunday heard sober, black-clad ministers fulminating above their heads for hours about hell and damnation, sailed off through the narrows on Monday on their lengthy voyages to buy or capture slaves on the West coast of Africa

Left: *Self portrait* by Rembrandt, as the Apostle Paul, with the sword, the attribute of St. Paul, thrust into the front of his coat and with a letter in his hand written in Hebrew characters.

Centre: *Portrait of Hendrickje Stoffels,* painted in 1654.

Right: *Portrait of Titus,* painted around 1660.

Baruch de Spinoza was born on 24 November 1632. He was the son of Michael and Hanna Debora de Spinoza, who had fled to Amsterdam from Vidigueira in Portugal. The Portuguese Jewish community had a school of its own: *Ets Chaim* (The Tree of Life). Its religious thought was dominated at that time by two rabbis: Rabbi Aboab, a conservative man, and Rabbi Menasseh ben Israel, a highly progressive theologian, philologist, printer and publisher, who lived opposite Rembrandt and was a friend of his and who later became famous as a statesman for his dealings with Cromwell, who opened England to the Jews again (1655-7). Spinoza received his first education at *Ets Chaim* in *Tenach* (the Bible), *Talmud* (the traditional interpretation of Jewish teaching) and, of course, Hebrew literature. He learnt Portuguese and Spanish from his earliest years, he made himself conversant with mathematics and the ex-Jesuit freethinker Franciscus van den Enden was his teacher in Greek and Latin. As a young man Spinoza, partly because of the religious contradictions in the community, became alienated from the traditional conceptions of God. What was more dangerous for the community, which, while it was certainly tolerated in Amsterdam, was nonetheless heavily dependent on the goodwill of the official Protestant

The doorway of the Anatomy Theatre in the Weigh-house on the New Market.

and sell them – in so far as they survived the journey – for a pound or two in the West. They were only blacks and heathens after all. And those same pious souls committed brutal murder on the victims of their privateering in order to bring their prizes back to their home ports with great jubilation. And they made no bones about forging coins on a large scale either. As a "solution" to social problems they treated the unemployed as a pack of knaves, condemning them to the house of correction or forced labour, since charitable help was no niggardly that they had no choice but to become beggars. This conjunction of opposites existed and continued to exist in spite of the earlier pleadings of a humane poet like Coornhert. God and money – that was, as an American historian has pithily summarized it, the basis of life in sixteenth- and seventeenth-century Holland.

That principle dominated the whole of the academic and literary life of the time. Theology was the most powerful of the academic disciplines and philology was derived from it to a large extent, while in law the emphasis fell on economic principles. Even the doctors of medicine had to take serious account of the overriding principle, for at this period, during which human anatomy became so important, bodies might only be dissected on rare occasions by the grace of the authorities and even then only the bodies of hanged criminals. When Rembrandt painted his famous *Anatomy Lessons* (those of Professor Tulp and Dr. Deyman), he gained his impressions for them during public lectures in the Weigh-house, a building that was thus dubbed "Carving Castle" at that time by Amsterdammers, who take such a keen delight in giving buildings nicknames.

But in spite of all that there was nonetheless a certain freedom. Roman Catholics (in reality the arch-enemies) were tolerated as long as they

church, was that he made no attempt to conceal his opinions. He came out openly for the view that people ought to interpret the Bible for themselves and not from the interpretations or traditions of others; that prescriptions relating to ritual are of no value if they are only based on tradition and that "people must look for piety and religion only in the practice of love and righteousness" (*Tractatus Theologico-Politicus,* published anonymously in Hamburg in 1670). These ideas constitued an attack not only on Jewish, but also on Protestant ways of thinking. It was as a result of all this that the great anathema was pronounced on him in the synagogue *Newé Sjaloom* (House of Peace) on

27 July 1656, after which the united church authorities expelled him from Amsterdam.

His philosophy, which is closely related to that of Descartes, was to set its stamp on the thinking of succeeding centuries. His most important works were a treatise on Descartes' philosophical principles and his *Ethica,* in which he demonstrated that God is the only being whose existence does not depend on anything else and whose being and existence are one. Man is part of the God who exists within him and around him and man's soul is bound up with his body, with all that that implies. In his third great work, the *Tractatus Theologico-Politicus,* Spinoza argued, among other things, for the separation of state and religion.

Menasseh ben Israel, a portrait etching made by Rembrandt in 1636.

In the 17th century the Dutch Republic was famous for its printed books. Great names of that time, such as Elsevier and Blaeu, still live on today. The refinement and taste the Dutch printer brought to his work is evinced by this title-page of a treatise on military architecture by Matthias Dögen, printed by "Elzevir" in Amsterdam in 1647 not only in Latin, but also in French and German. The book, an excellent manual for the military architect, was reprinted many times.

MATTHIÆ DÖGEN
Dramburgensis Marchici
ARCHITECTVRA
MILITARIS MODERNA
Varijs Hiftorijs, tam veteribus quam novis confirmata, et præcipuis totius Europæ munimentis, ad exemplum adductis exornata.

AMSTELODAMI,
Apud Ludovicum Elzevirium. Anno 1647

held their services in concealed churches and did not propagate their faith. Mennonites led a relatively safe existence and even the followers of the extreme free thinker, Faustus Socinus, an Italian who eventually settled in Poland, found a refuge there when they were driven out of Poland and Germany. Did Rembrandt come into contact with the Socinians? That we do not know for certain, although some think his famous etching *Dr. Faustus* could be an indication that he did so. His work does, however, prove beyond a doubt that he had contact with the Jews, who had been in Amsterdam since the end of the sixteenth century, although they were not allowed to acquire citizenship rights any more than any other dissenting groups. In particular Rembrandt was closely associated with the often very unorthodox Jewish rabbi Menasseh ben Israel, who lived opposite him and for whose theological treatise, *The Glorious Stone,* he even made four etchings.

Notwithstanding all that might be said against it, Rembrandt's Amsterdam was a liberal city – cosmopolitan through its trade, crowded with foreigners from all over the world, full of churches and fairs, taverns and workplaces, poets and painters, rich men and paupers. Altogether it numbered around a hundred and twenty thousand inhabitants, who were undoubtedly very conscious of the fact that they lived in a city that was the centre of the seventeenth-century world.

The Round Luteran Church on the Singel, built between 1668 and 1671 after a disign by Adriaan Dortsman. A painting by Jacob Storck.

Two and a half centuries of the Nightwatch

1642 to 1885 – from *Kloveniersdoelen* to Rijksmuseum – changing evaluation

As far as we know Rembrandt's *Nightwatch* was to its contemporaries a painting like any other, not exceptionally beautiful, but not exceptionally ugly, extravagant or unorthodox either. Nor do we know of any contemporary opinions about the painting any more than we have commentaries on the other militia pieces in the great hall of the *Kloveniersdoelen*. The first comment of any length on the *Nightwatch* dates from 1678 *i.e.* 35 years or so after it was painted. In his *Introduction to the High School of Painting*, Samuel van Hoogstraten, who at one time was a pupil of Rembrandt's, wrote of the *Nightwatch* that it is not enough that a painter should arrange all the persons in a painting next to each other in rows, as can often be seen in Holland in militia pieces. A good painter takes care to see that his picture forms a unity. This Rembrandt has certainly done in his painting in the Doelen, all too well, in the opinion of some people, "making more work of the great composition of his own devising than of the individual portraits that were commissioned

A Meeting of the Patriots in the Great Hall of the Kloveniersdoelen in 1748. The engraver has depicted the hall as if the militia pieces were still hanging there, but they had actually already been transferred to the Town Hall in 1715. He has further made a mistake in showing four paintings instead of three on the long wall.

The Doelen Hotel, built on the site of the *Kloveniersdoelen*.

As the useful function of the militia receded more and more into the background in the 17th century, so their guildhalls came to be used for celebrations and as hotel accommodation. The city council also organized banquets there for important visitors. In 1816 the *Kloveniersdoelen* was let to a publican, J.H. Brack, who made it into a hotel, converting the firing range on the opposite side of the street into a bath-house. The *Swijgh Utrecht* Tower was finally pulled down in 1882 to make way for the building of the Doelen Hotel on the site. In the façade of the Amstel side of the Hotel the architect tried to preserve the effect of the original construction with the projecting round tower and the straight front of the great hall. A stone tablet with a depiction of the *Swijgh Utrecht* Tower was set in the façade of the hotel near the bridge.

from him. But that same work, no matter how much it can be criticised, will to my mind outlive all its competitors, since it is so painterly in conception, so dashing in movement and so powerful that, according to some, all the other pieces there look like playing-cards beside it". In 1686 the Italian Filippo Baldinucci wrote a book about famous engravers and etchers in which he included Rembrandt. In his book he also gave some information about Rembrandt as a painter, which he probably got from the Danish painter Bernhardt Keil, who had been a pupil of Rembrandt's between 1642 and 1644. Among other things, he wrote of the *Nightwatch* that it was greatly admired because a captain (he meant the lieutenant) appeared on it with a spontoon in his hand of which the perspective was so perfectly painted that it seems just as if you saw the shaft at its full length. People had a great feeling for such "absolutely real" effects in the seventeenth century. Stories are legion about painters who could paint something so realistically that the spectator no longer knew where reality ended and the painting began, which sometimes led to comical mistakes. All the same Baldinucci (and evidently his informant Keil too) thought that the rest of the painting was too dark and confusing. It was as a result of remarks such as this and those of Van Hoogstraten

Festive performance on the Amstel near the *Kloveniersdoelen* on the occasion of the visit of a Muscovite legation to Amsterdam on 29 August 1697. On the left is the *Doelen* building where the City Council held a banquet for the legation in the evening. (p. 86, bottom).

The fire at the old Town Hall on 7 July 1652. The Town Hall was burned right down to the ground. A start had already been made on building the new Town Hall in 1648, but it was not possible to move into it until 1655. The maker of this print, Jan van der Heyden, was also the inventor of a fire-engine and on the right of the print he shows how much less human exertion is needed to extinguish a fire if his engine is used.

In 1658-9, at the request of the guardian of Rembrandt's son, Titus, an enquiry was initiated into Rembrandt's property before the death of his wife Saskia on 14 June 1642. On behalf of that enquiry two militiamen of the *Kloveniersdoelen* made statements in the presence of Notary Listingh as to the sums they had paid Rembrandt in 1642 for the group portrait in the *Doelen*. The text of one of these declarations reads as follows: "Mr. Jan Pietersz (Bronchorst), draper, aged about seventy years, appeared and...has...by true Christian words in place of the oath attested, deposed and certified how that it is true that he, the attestant, was painted and portrayed by Rembrandt van Rhijn, painter, alongside other persons of their company to a total number of sixteen in a painting now standing in the great hall of the *Kloveniersdoelen* and that each of them, according to the memory he the attestant still has of it, had paid for the painting on average the sum of a hundred guilders, the one a little more, the other a little less according to the place he had in it." These declarations were, therefore, meant as evidence of Rembrandt's earnings of before 14 June 1642. They show that the *Nightwatch* had been paid for and must thus have been completed before that date.

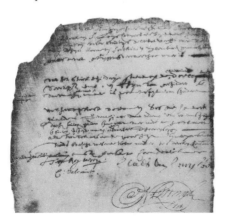

that the myth came into being later on in the 19th century that the *Nightwatch* was rejected by the people who had commissioned it or even, according to some versions of the story, banished to a dark attic.

In considering all the criticism levelled at Rembrandt's work at the end of the seventeenth and during the eighteenth century, it is important to remember that that criticism arose at a period when ideas about what a good work of art ought to look like had changed radically from those of Rembrandt's day. The criticism was thus often the result of the application of contemporary standards to the artistic productions of a previous generation. And since Rembrandt was the greatest artist of that previous generation, he naturally came in for the most criticism.

The artists of the end of the seventeenth century regarded it as highly important that anyone engaged in art should have a sound theoretical background, that he should know the rules of art, especially those of anatomy and perspective. Looked at from that point of view the art of Rembrandt and his contemporaries, who placed application and practice above rules and who thought that ugly things could also be worth painting, was reprehensible. The only explanation people could think of for the fact that an artist had defied the rules to such an extent was that he must have been a person who had set his face against order and established society in general. And so was born, years after his death, Rembrandt the rebel painter, the "first heretic in painting", as he was also called, a Rembrandt of whom it is highly questionable, to say the least, whether he bore any resemblance to the "real" Rembrandt.

But what made Rembrandt objectionable in the eyes of the art critics of the late seventeenth and the eighteenth centuries, albeit they had to allow that he was a great artist, was precisely what made him the most revered of all painters in the nineteenth century. In the Romantic era an artist who rebelled against the established rules, who had to suffer in order to produce art in his own way, was actually regarded as a greater artist than one who fitted in with the taste of his time.

So it was that for the Romantics Rembrandt became the model of what an artist ought to be and that he could begin to play a role as a national hero, alongside William the Silent and Admiral De Ruyter. Also connected with this was the fact that in the second quarter of the nineteenth century a need was felt for an artist who could determine the unique vision of the Netherlands. After the dismal failure of the union between Holland and Belgium in 1830, Holland began a search for its own identity and so Rembrandt was gratefully seized on as an artist who could salve and restore the wounded national pride again, in competition with Rubens, the national painter of Belgium. From this period stem the plans for the setting up of a bronze statue of Rembrandt on the Butter Market (now Rembrandtsplein) in Amsterdam, although the statue, a cast-iron one, was not actually put there until 1852.

When plans began being made in the eighteen-sixties for the building of a new and perfect home for the national art treasures, which at that time were miserably housed, thoughts naturally also turned to installing Rembrandt's paintings in a way that would do them honour. In the design eventually adopted for the new Rijksmuseum Rembrandt's *Nightwatch* was even given a central place, becoming

The Dam, with, on the left, the new Town Hall, the "eighth wonder of the world" in course of building. On the right can be seen the Damrak, which at that time had not yet been filled in and to which ships conveyed the goods that were sold on the Dam (p.88).

The new Town Hall in all its glory, painted by Gerrit Berckheyde in 1693. In 1715 the *Nightwatch* was to come to hang on the first floor at the back in the Small Court Martial Chamber. The Weigh-house (on the right) was pulled down in 1808 on the orders of King Louis Napoleon.

This is the famous copy of the *Night-watch* that has been attributed to Gerrit Lundens. It is famous primarily for its accuracy and for the fact that the strips later cut off the top and left-hand side of the painting are still to be seen on it. The copy belongs to the National Gallery in London, but since 1952 it has hung in the *Night-watch* room in the Rijksmuseum.

more or less the pivot on which the entire museum turned.

The national collection was in fact very badly off around 1870 as far as paintings by Rembrandt were concerned. The Rijksmuseum had only three Rembrandts: *The Nightwatch, The Syndics* and *The Jewish Bride* and all of them were on loan from the city of Amsterdam. The city's collection of paintings consisted to a large extent of the portraits that had formerly hung in all sorts of public buildings, such as the *Doelen,* the Orphanages and the Guildhalls. Toward the

The Trippenhuis on the Kloveniersburgwal, which in 1815 was made into the Rijksmuseum of paintings, coins and medals. The *Night-watch* also acquired a place there at that time. It had already hung there earlier, in 1808, when the Town Hall on the Dam had had to be cleared of its contents for King Louis Napoleon.

90

end of the seventeenth century, when the militia had more or less ceased to function, the *Doelen* buildings came to be used more and more for public meetings. The *Kloveniersdoelen* was used for festivities and as a hotel and auction rooms and the paintings suffered somewhat from all these activities. For this reason it was decided in 1715 to transfer the paintings from the *Kloveniersdoelen* to the Town Hall on the Dam. There seven militia pieces, including the *Nightwatch,* were hung in the Small Court-Martial Chamber. The *Nightwatch* was just a bit too big for the place allotted to it, so it was simply made smaller. A piece was cut off all round or perhaps first folded back and then cut off later.

Visitors occasionally came to look at the paintings in the Town Hall. Among them was the English painter, Sir Joshua Reynolds, who came in 1781. He was a great admirer of Rembrandt, but he was not particularly taken with the *Nightwatch*. He wrote in his travel diary: "So far indeed am I from thinking that this last picture deserves its great reputation, that it was with difficulty I could persuade myself that is was painted by Rembrandt; it seemed to me to have more of the yellow manner of [Ferdinand] Bol".

In 1808 the Town Hall was placed at the disposal of King Louis Napoleon as a palace and the paintings were transferred pell-mell to a large house on the Kloveniersburgwal, the Trippenhuis. Then Louis Napoleon decided to turn two rooms in the palace into museum galleries, the first beginnings of a National Museum. Along with a number of other paintings the *Nightwatch* was selected to form part of this museum. After the departure of Louis Napoleon and the fall of Napoleon, the Palace was offered to King William I and the paintings in the two museum galleries were moved to the Trippen-

The Statue of Rembrandt on Rembrandtsplein in Amsterdam. It was designed by Louis Royer in 1852.

The *Nightwatch* in the Trippenhuis in 1872, a painting by August Jernberg.

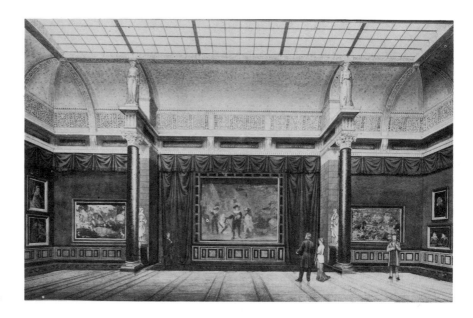

Design for the *Nightwatch* room, 1881.

The *Nightwatch* extension, c. 1910.

huis, which was then given the name Rijksmuseum. Conditions there were far from ideal for the paintings and this Rijksmuseum came to be dubbed the "National Dump".

Plans for a new building had already begun to take shape in 1863, but not until 1885 was it possible for the new museum building to be officially opened. The architect of the enormous complex was Dr. P.H.J. Cuypers. He had sited the paintings galleries on the first floor around two inner courts. Between them in the centre lay the Gallery of Honour, which led directly into the room where the *Nightwatch* was to be hung. The whole room was a glorification of Rembrandt, with texts about his life round the walls and his monogram in the mosaics on the floor. The vaulted roof was supported by four statues representing *Morning, Day, Evening* and *Night*. But in

The *Nightwatch* room, c. 1935.

The *Nightwatch* room in 1959. The room was rebuilt once again in 1976-7.

practice the room proved unsatisfactory. The enormous amount of daylight that came in through the glass ceiling and was reflected by the light floor made the *Nightwatch* seem all too dark once more. Attempts were made to remedy this by hanging a velvet canopy in the room, but even that was not satisfactory.

Not until 1898, when the *Nightwatch* was lent to a large Rembrandt exhibition in the Stedelijk Museum and as a result suddenly appeared to much better advantage again, did people begin to think the solution had been found: the painting ought to be lit from the side. Tests were carried out in a wooden shed on Museumplein and in 1905 it was decided to build a new Rembrandt room behind the old one and with sidelighting. This room was opened with great ceremony in the Rembrandt anniversary year 1906. But here too the installation

The *Nightwatch* "goes into hiding". Leaving the museum in 1939.

21 March 1941: The *Nightwatch*, rolled up, being carried into a bunker near Heemskerk.

25 June 1945: the *Nightwatch* on its way back to Amsterdam.

The Rijksmuseum around 1890 (p.95).

proved unsatisfactory in practice and in 1922 the *Nightwatch* was taken back to its original room. There it was hung on a different wall, while the other evils were remedied as far as possible by a dark floor covering and a false ceiling.

The threat of war in 1939 made it necessary for the *Nightwatch* to "go into hiding". It was transferred to Radboud Castle at Medemblik. On 13 and 14 May 1940 it was moved to a bunker at Castricum, where it was removed from its stretcher and rolled up round a cylinder with the paint layer on the outside, just as it had probably made the journey three centuries before from Rembrandt's studio to the *Kloveniersdoelen*. Yet another removal, to a bunker at Heemskerk, took place on 21 March 1941 and a year later, on 24 March 1942, the painting was taken to a bunker in the St. Pieterberg near Maastricht. About six weeks after the liberation, on 25 June 1945, it travelled back to Amsterdam and by the end of July it was once more on view in the Rijksmuseum.

For a hundred years or so now the *Nightwatch* has been one of the most famous paintings in the world and it does not look as if that is likely to change in the near future, certainly not since the recent restoration. Whether it is also one of the most beautiful paintings in the world is a question of taste and, as we know, opinions may differ on this point.

The name *Nightwatch* came into being around 1800. It is a nickname for a dark painting of a group of militiamen, which had actually become a great deal darker over the years. Before then all sorts of names were in use, but they were really more like descriptions than titles, *e.g. The Doelen Piece by Rembrandt* or *A Company of Militiamen on the March.* The first explicit use of the name *Nightwatch* occurs in 1808 in the correspondence about the transfer of the painting from the Town Hall on the Dam to the Trippenhuis, but in the first catalogue of the National Museum, published in 1809, it is stated that the painting is known all over the world as the *Nightwatch,* which suggests that the name must already have been in use before 1808, although no examples of its use are known. Even now, even after the restoration when the painting is as light as it was when Rembrandt painted it, it is still quite dark by comparison with the other militia pieces from the Great Hall of the *Kloveniersdoelen,* in which the militiamen are lit by a cool, even light. This is because Rembrandt wanted to give expression to the dramatic element in his painting in the play of light and dark as well.

The knife and the new light

the attack of 14 September 1975 – restoration in the past and now –
– the restoration

On the afternoon of Sunday 14 September 1975 the doors of the Rijksmuseum opened at one o'clock just as they do on any other Sunday afternoon. The people who had been waiting to go in paid their admission fees and the vast majority of them set off at once up the wide staircase leading to the first floor. There are to be found the rooms that attract far and away the most visitors, those of Dutch seventeenth-century painting. Everyone who walks through those rooms – it is a "one way system" – comes to the place where the *Nightwatch* has hung since 1885 as the cornerstone of this great hey-day of Dutch painting. There he also stands in the heart of the museum, for Cuypers, the architect, literally built it around that room between 1876 and 1885. In Cuypers' eyes – and not only his – the *Nightwatch* marked the apex of Rembrandt's powers and Rembrandt the apex of Dutch art.

Among the visitors that Sunday was a tallish, unobtrusive man who

Not only does the *Nightwatch* hang at a central point in the Rijksmuseum, but it is also for many visitors the high point of their tour of the rooms where the masterpieces of Dutch 17th-century painting hang – a high point and a point of rest at the same time, however many visitors the Rijksmuseum has to cope with each year. Recently they have numbered getting on for a million and a half per year, most of them coming to the museum in the summer months and during the Christmas holidays.

hurried through the rooms and came to a halt in the *Nightwatch* room, where he looked for a moment or two at Van der Helst's militia piece, *The Company of Captain Roelof Bicker*. As on every other day in the year, there was a warder standing by the Persian carpet on the floor in front of the *Nightwatch*. The carpet marked an invisible barrier between the painting and the public: you could come up to the *Nightwatch* so far, but no further. Also standing there was a girl who had likewise come in early on and was looking at the *Nightwatch* which up to then she had known only from reproductions. Obliquely behind her, in a corner of the room, her fiancé was looking at the copy of the *Nightwatch* attributed to Gerrit Lundens. The visitor in front of the Van der Helst suddenly turned round, strode up to the *Nightwatch* and stepped on to the carpet. At the very moment when the warder called out to him, "Step back from that carpet please, sir", he pulled out a knife with a serrated edge with his left hand. It was three minutes past one. With lightning speed and unimaginable force the man stabbed at the canvas with the knife, slashing long cuts in it. The warder sprang at him and tried to drag him away from the *Nightwatch*. The girl screamed, feeling that she was threatened too. Her fiancé raced up to the man, jumped at him from behind and, with one arm round his throat, dragged him and the warder away from the painting. Warders came rushing in from neighbouring rooms. The knife fell to the ground, wrenched crooked by the force of the stabbing. A yard or two away lay a triangle of canvas, 28 centimetres high and 6 centimetres wide at the base, that had been cut out of the painting. The man, overpowered and suddenly much quieter now, was led away to the Superintendent's office. The *Nightwatch* seemed to have been damaged beyond repair by twelve scratches and cuts, seven of which had gone right through the canvas and the relining canvas. It had all happened in a few seconds – less time than it has taken you to read this.

The room soon filled with visitors who poured in to stand looking at the ravaged painting in dead silence, bewilderment and, curiously,

The head of the militiaman on the *Nightwatch* after restoration was completed.

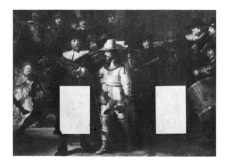

The cuts and scratches were given a coating of resin, so that it could be seen exactly where the cuts were and where only the varnish had been damaged. Pieces of mulberry paper were pasted over the cuts to prevent the canvas from sagging.

The painting laid down with the paint side downwards. The wooden stretcher has been removed. The cuts and other (old) damage have been marked on the relining canvas in chalk.

The militiaman behind Van Ruytenburch, cleaned, but not yet varnished and retouched (left).

Below: microphotograph of the shoulder on the left. The yellowish patches top left are retouching. The rest of the paint appeared, in spite of the difference in colour, to be entirely by Rembrandt himself.

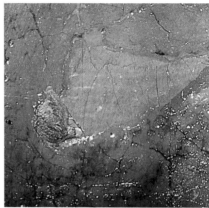

A primary requirement in the restoring of paintings is to get as clear as possible a picture of the composition of the paint layer. The microscope has been used to investigate this for a long while now. During the restoration of the *Nightwatch*, too, many microscopical (coloured) photographs were made of those parts of the canvas where retouching was needed. Photographs of this type are popularly known as microphotographs, because they give a greatly enlarged image (in the photographs here an enlargement of 16 times).

The relining canvas that had been applied at the restoration of 1946 was pulled away from Rembrandt's canvas. A broad strip of it was left in place round the edges.

The cuts were joined together with short threads drawn from unprepared painters' canvas. These threads were dripped in epoxy resin (synthetic resin) and laid over the cuts. When the resin had hardened, the ends of the linen threads were pared smooth.

From the official report on the damage made on 14 September 1975: "The painting was cut 12 times with a knife, the cuts varying in length from 100 to 39 cm". Some cuts had only gone through the original canvas, causing it to fray, but having been deflected by the relining canvas; others had cut through the original canvas and the relining canvas. At the place of the knife cuts themselves and, of course, along the edges, there was considerable loss of paint, the more because the total picture there gave the impression that: 1. the stabs and cuts had been inflicted with great force; 2. the blade of the knife had been bent slightly to the left, probably as a result of the force and speed of the blows; some of the cuts were pressed obliquely inwards and all the cut edges were frayed. In addition, a number of white stripes were also visible, where the knife had been deflected by the paint and where, therefore, only the varnish was damaged.

As a result of the uncontrolled cutting a triangular piece of canvas with paint (28 x 6 cm) had fallen out of the painting. To the left of this a complicated break (3 cm wide) had been occasioned; because of the falling away of the triangular piece this break had resulted in the paint layer on the original canvas coming away from the relining canvas and curling upwards and downwards. Two other breaks in the paint layer, the grounding and the original canvas had also been caused by the brute force.

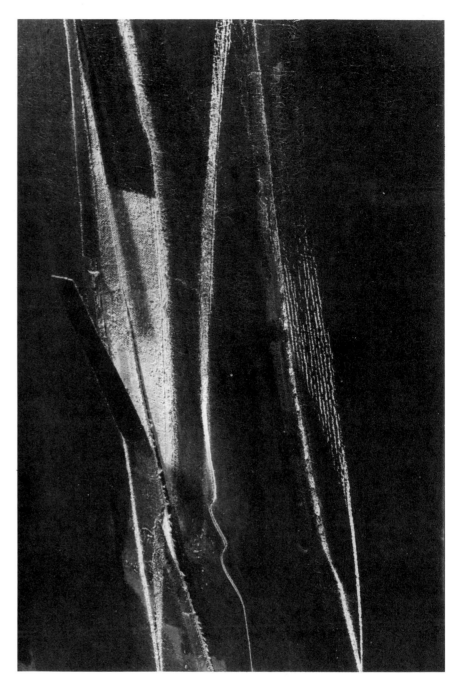

Pieces of plastic film and small sandbags were placed on the repaired cuts, so that the resin would harden under pressure.

Sheets of softboard were fastened to the stretcher, which was then laid on the back of the painting. The edges of the relining canvas were folded over the stretcher and secured to it with laths.

100

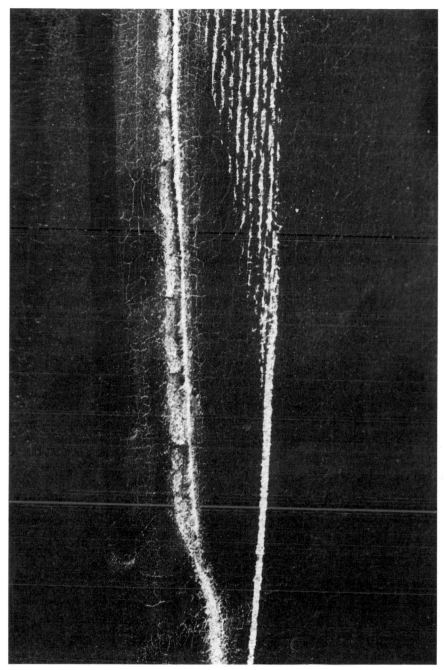

Because there were knife cuts 85 cm long, which had gone through both the original canvas and the relining canvas, and because they were relatively close together, it was necessary to reline the whole painting again. Because of the paint loss along both sides of the cuts and the scraping away of the varnish down to the paint layer in places, it was necessary to remove the whole of the varnish layer.

Far left: the cuts in Banning Cocq's breeches. The light part is the relining canvas; a piece of Rembrandt's canvas has fallen off there.

Left: the cut in Banning Cocq's right leg.

Below: the cuts near the dog.

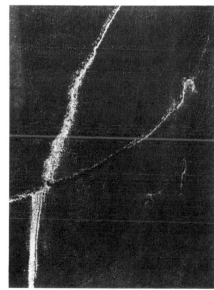

The painting is turned over. The bands of webbing were there to ensure that the canvas could not flap about while being turned over and that nothing serious could happen when the old canvas was cut away from the strip of relining canvas.

The webbing bands have been removed. The border of relining canvas has been cut through along the stretcher and the narrow bands of relining canvas still remaining under the painting carefully pulled away.

The militiaman in red on the *Night-watch*, cleaned, but not yet varnished and retouched (right).
The militiaman in red now (above).

The *Nightwatch* was pasted over with broad bands of paper that were taken round a wooden loom of larger dimensions than the painting. This was done with a cellulose paste.

The *Nightwatch* completely pasted over with paper. It can still be seen through the paper, as the paste has not yet dried.

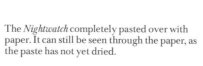

Sergeant Reinicr Engelen, cleaned, but not yet varnished (left). Reinier Engelen now (above). His face was so little damaged that retouching was not necessary. The aim of the restorer is, after all, not to repair a painting completely, but to ensure that no disturbing defects can be seen from a normal viewing distance.

Bands of canvas were stretched over the paper to prevent the *Nightwatch* from flapping about too much while it was being turned over. After it had been turned, the bands were carefully drawn away from underneath.

The *Nightwatch* is turned over in the loom. A supporting lath has been applied to the back of the loom to prevent the painting from sagging.

The value of a schedule as an aid in the restoration of a large painting has already been proven many times in the past. During the process of a restoration there has to be a great deal of improvisation, often at moments when it is necessary to take decisions immediately. If the problems that might possibly arise have been indicated beforehand in a schedule, that makes it easier to take a quick decision. Again, the painting has, for example, to be turned over many times during the course of restoration and its dimensions will continually differ in this as a result of the auxiliary wooden frames that have to be placed around it. If a single procedure were to be forgotten, it could mean having to turn the painting over even more.

When a tear or a cut is made in a canvas, this means that that canvas no longer exists and reacts as a single entity. Depending on climatological conditions the fibres in the canvas on either side of the cut or tear can start to react differently. Thus it is advisable to repair the damage as quickly as possible, even if only provisionally sometimes, and to put the canvas in order again, so that it can react as a single unit in all conceivable circumstances.

The same goes for a panel. Once it is split or broken, then it must be glued together again within the shortest possible time, because otherwise the two parts can work loose from each other and it will only be possible to join them invisibly with the greatest difficulty.

from a distance, as if they dared not go nearer. Fifteen minutes later screens hurriedly brought from elsewhere in the museum had been placed in front of the damaged lower part of the *Nightwatch* to form an improvised wall, which was flanked by two warders. Around four o'clock that afternoon the authorities of the Rijksmuseum were able, after a first rapid inspection, to announce to a hastily summoned press conference that, although the *Nightwatch* was indeed very severely damaged, it was not irreparably so. The restoration would, as far as could be estimated, take around four and a half to five months. In fact the restoration actually began early the next morning. The fresh wounds in the painting were desperately in need of "first aid"; in particular, a piece of canvas that had been cut loose in the centre had in the course of a few hours come to hang so far forward that there was a very real danger of it breaking away. First aid for paintings can, like that for human beings, be extremely simple. Those parts of the canvas that threatened to curl up or even break off were stuck together on the back of the painting with a few pieces of ordinary adhesive tape. The *Nightwatch*, sadly battered though it was, was now reasonably safe in the circumstances. It would at any rate be able to survive the first weeks without harm.

And so began yet another restoration of one of the most famous paintings in the world. For the umpteenth time strange hands were needed to bring the canvas back to a presentabe state again. It had had a good deal to suffer in the 323 years of its existence. Up to the moment of the new attack more than sixty places had been counted where it had been damaged, sometimes only very lightly, sometimes quite heavily and on one occasion, when it was placed in the Small Court-Martial Chamber in the Town Hall, irreparably for all time.

What is "restoration"? Both the word and the profession of restorer are very recent in their modern meanings. At present the situation is that the restoration is done in a scientific manner, each step being

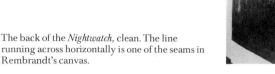
The adhesive remaining from previous relinings is removed.

The back of the *Nightwatch*, clean. The line running across horizontally is one of the seams in Rembrandt's canvas.

documented by reports, photographs, X-ray photographs and what have you, but there was no question of that in the past. In so far as any reports were made, they were summary in the extreme, generally containing little more than a bald statement of the fact that something had been done to a work of art. The profession of restorer passed, as with so many other crafts, from father to son, from teacher to apprentice. The methods were mostly regarded as of minor

A relining frame with the new canvas, a single piece, has been placed inside the loom. The cross laths in that frame are moveable. A warm mixture of beeswax and resin is being brushed into the relining canvas. This mixture solidifies almost immediately.

The wax-resin mixture is melted again with a warm iron, so that it penetrates through the canvas enabling Rembrandt's canvas to stick to the relining canvas.

The first stage in the regeneration of the varnish: Banning Cocq's legs appear again out of the varnish that had become opaque.

The *Nightwatch*, cut out of the loom is turned over again.

The front, pasted over with paper, comes to lie upwards again.

importance: only the results mattered and the secrets of the trade never left the studio. Nowadays the restorer is exceptionally scrupulous, but less secretive. Moreover, he feels himself very much bound by the period and the style in which an old master worked. But this feeling is one that was only gradually arrived at during the second half of the nineteenth century. Before that time the approach to "freshening-up" a work of art was quite different.

As far as we know that "freshening-up" began at a very early date. Even before the sixteenth century damaged works of art were being entrusted to artists like Lorenzo di Credi, the Bellinis and others for repair. Gossaert and Frans Hals are also known to have restored pictures, but nothing is known about how they did it. There are some well-known examples. It is, for instance, an established fact that Jan van Scorel and Lancelot Blondeel restored, repaired or,

The face of the drummer Jan van Kampoort before and after restoration (left and above respectively).

A tense moment: the paper is torn off. How has the *Nightwatch* stood up to the relining?

All the most important moments in the restoration were filmed. Here the restorers are engaged on removing the last pieces of paper and inspecting the varnish layer.

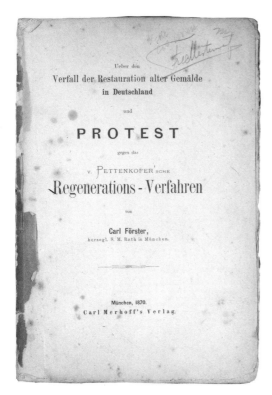

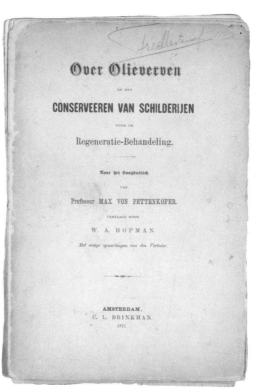

Dutch translation of the book of 1870 on methods of regeneration with alcohol vapours by Max von Pettenkofer (right). Protest against the Von Pettenkofer method published by Carl Förster in 1870 (left).

probably better still, "freshened up" Jan van Eyck's famous *Adoration of the Lamb*. They were both extremely skilled painters, but they did not scruple to alter or add details in accordance with their own ideas, something that came to be held against them later on.

It was, however, customary at that time for a painter doing restoration work to alter certain details according to his own ideas and by so doing to give the original work of art an aspect never intended by its creator. In this people were governed by the tastes and modes of their own day, knowing little or nothing of that respect for the original that is the basis of all restoration work nowadays. A tremendous amount of work must have been done in this way. In the seventeenth century, for example, painters would be put in charge of important collections and this included their conservation and, of

Banning Cocq's leg. The places where the cuts were, which were already pasted over with paper on the first day, have become virtually completely invisible.

The varnish layer has become completely opaque as a result of the action of the cellulose paste with which the paper was stuck down and because of remains of paper. The restorer is making the varnish transparent again by regenerating it with alchohol.

course, restoration. Towards the end of the century we already find mention being made in inventories of the relining of paintings. At the beginning of the eighteenth century the craft of restoring begins to exhibit some refinements. Three specialist fields had already come into being by then: first, relining; secondly, the transferring of the paint layer to a new support (canvas or panel), and finally, the application of cradling. In the middle of the eighteenth century one finds descriptions of the technique of relining. Originally glue was used for this, but later on – around 1850 – the so-called "Dutch method" came into favour, which was based on a mixture of wax and resin. By that time doubts were already being cast on the efficacy of cradling (a method whereby people tried to strengthen a panel and protect it from the influence of humidity by supporting laths), yet it still continued to be used here and there, even though it was for the most part abandoned. It gradually also became known that retouching done with oil paint could darken with time and so areas where new paint was needed were then generally done a fraction lighter in order to allow for this effect.

In the nineteenth century it came to be realised that tradition is not always reliable after all. People became aware of the importance of good, genuine restoration and they began to think about methods and to invent new procedures. That was the period of regeneration with alcohol (Max von Pettenkofer, 1818-1901), of the deliberate use of coloured varnishes (to achieve the so-called "Gallery Varnish") and the method invented in the Netherlands of relining paintings by using wax and resin. A great deal of experimentation was done at that time. For example, attempts were made to remove varnish layers by "powdering", without making use of chemicals, but the results proved so disastrous that this method was pretty soon given up again. What people were after in those days was the achievement of complete integration: damaged or not, a painting had to be completely retouched, even if, to our way of thinking now, retouching was only needed in a very few places.

A properly planned system of documentation in a restoration studio ought to contain photographs made before, during and after a restoration, including photographs taken under a strong, raking light and with ultra-violet and infra-red filters, X-ray photographs and microphotographs. In addition there should be a detailed description of the entire procedure, including the chemicals, the types of adhesive and other materials used. Here brand names should be avoided, as they are all too subject to alteration. Microscopical observations must be clearly described, likewise the results of chemical analyses of paint and other examinations, along with the restorer's own interpretation of them. It is also extremely important to describe the condition of the painting before restoration and the reasons why the restoration was necessary.

A paint layer characterized by impasto can be pressed flat during relining as a result of the use of heat. This has often happened when relining has not been properly carried out. If a painting on canvas is laid down on a heated surface, then the paint becomes warm and takes on the structure of the canvas.

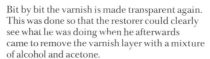
The *Nightwatch* in an upright position again.

Bit by bit the varnish is made transparent again. This was done so that the restorer could clearly see what he was doing when he afterwards came to remove the varnish layer with a mixture of alcohol and acetone.

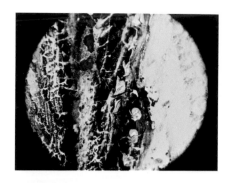

Microphotograph of the tassel on Van Ruytenburch's spontoon, taken in order to get an idea of the composition of the blue colour (above).

Microphotograph of the foreground near the feet of the militiaman in red (below).

Not until this century did people really become fully aware of the importance of good, responsible restoration, which means, to put it briefly, carrying out only as much restoration and retouching as is absolutely necessary and, if humanly possible, doing it in such a way that the restoration work done today can be removed again, so to say, tomorrow, or after a year or two, or after a generation, without the restored work being damaged in any way as a result.

Naturally there are good and bad restorers – it is no different from any other profession – but it has become a profession with a sober, scientific basis. And that means that nowadays people do not hesitate in cases of extreme difficulty to call on experts in all sorts of disciplines, who are often brought together in international committees. That was done, for example, at the restoration of the *Adoration of the Lamb* and the *Mona Lisa* and, very recently, of Vermeer's *Love Letter*. In the case of the *Nightwatch* such a committee proved unnecessary, but grateful use was nonetheless made of the

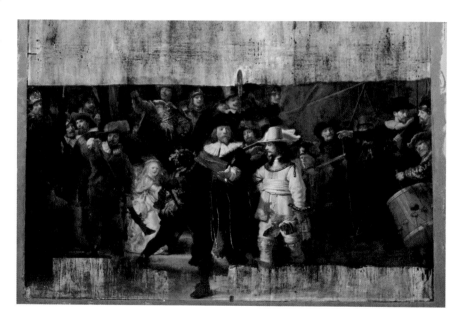

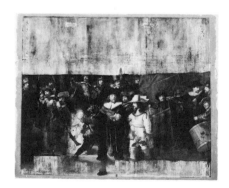

Half-way through the cleaning process. The cuts are already much less noticeable, even though they have not yet been retouched at all.

After cleaning the *Nightwatch* was carefully examined with the microscope.

110

The restorer engaged on retouching.

The signature on the *Nightwatch: Rembrandt f 1642.* The f stands for the Latin word *fecit* (he made it).

advice of experts from outside the Rijksmuseum.

The new and most far-reaching restoration ever to be undergone by the *Nightwatch* had now begun. When the most badly damaged places had been temporarily secured on the back with adhesive tape, those places were pasted over on the front with mulberry paper after they had been partly degreased with xylene. After that there was little else for the restorers to do for a time, apart from preparing their work on paper.

But in those first two weeks – up to 29 September – a great many changes had to be made in the room. It was impossible to restore

Use was made of the opportunity to inspect old areas of damage and work on them if necessary. Here is an old "stopping".

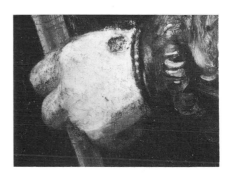

The hole in the drummer's hand.

The relining canvas used in the restoration of 1975-6 was made of a single piece of material. Rembrandt himself did not have such a large piece of canvas at his disposal. He had to have three lengths of canvas sewn together horizontally to achieve the format of the picture commissioned from him. During the restoration the seams of these lengths of canvas were clearly to be seen, especially on the back of the painting. In several places at the edges they had even come undone and they had to be stuck together in the way described above. Loose threads remaining from this process were removed before relining in order to prevent them being pressed through to make an impression on the surface of the painting.

No attention is ever paid to the seams in a painted canvas, but this is a great mistake. It is in fact very important to do so, since it appears that the pieces of canvas sewn together are always of equal width. These equal proportions of the lengths of canvas are of great importance to the painter who has to work on that canvas. If one comes across a painted canvas of which the pieces sewn together are different from one another, then that could indicate that a correction or alteration has been made at a later date.

the painting anywhere else in the museum but in the *Nightwatch* room. The rapidly created *Nightwatch* committee at once took a decision that was to cause a sensation the world over: the painting would be restored in full view of the public. Thus a wall had to be built in the room, behind which the restoration could take place and in which five large windows were made. Obviously the restorers would have to be able to work in the greatest possible peace and quiet and that they would do behind closed curtains, but as soon as they had finished their work for the day, the curtains were drawn back, so that people could see what stage had been reached. And because a good many of the procedures were incomprehensible to the layman, the Education Service of the Rijksmuseum set up in an adjacent room an exhibition in the form of a wall newspaper, in which the various stages in the work were explained in pictures and words (in Dutch and English). In the course of the succeeding months it was to become an exhibition that attracted many hundreds of thousands of visitors.

Still more provisions were required for the restoration. Because the canvas would have to lie on the ground for a large part of the time, a work floor ten centimetres high was built and over it a movable work bridge which made it possible for the restorers to reach any part of the painting with ease. New apparatus was brought in as well: an extractor unit to remove dust and noxious vapours, daylight lamps and new X-ray equipment. At the same time and in close collaboration with the municipality of Amsterdam, the owner of the *Nightwatch,* the radical decision was taken to remove not only the new layer of varnish that had been applied in 1947, but also the remains of older varnish layers that were still present on the painting. The *Nightwatch* had not received any "treatment" during the preceding 28 years, something made possible by the expert way the new varnish had been applied in 1947, but that varnish, which had a mastic basis, had nonetheless become brittle and had begun to

Abrasion on Banning Cocq's face.

Where paint was missing, a brown stopping was used in order to make the level up to that of Rembrandt's paint layer. This stopping remains flexible and can easily be removed should it ever be necessary.

powder here and there. Thus, now that it had in any case been so badly damaged, a complete cleaning seemed the obvious course to take.

In the first week of October, then, the real work of restoration began. The *Nightwatch* was taken out of its frame and the damage was thoroughly inspected once again, with the aid of strong photoflood lamps. The varnish layer appeared to be quite thick in most places, but over the figure of Van Ruytenburch it proved relatively thin, a necessary piece of knowledge for what had to be done later. Meanwhile the work floor had been covered with a layer of felt and plastic sheeting. The *Nightwatch* was laid on it with the paint

The chief restorer of the Rijksmuseum, H.H. Mertens, engaged on the 1946-7 restoration of the *Nightwatch*.

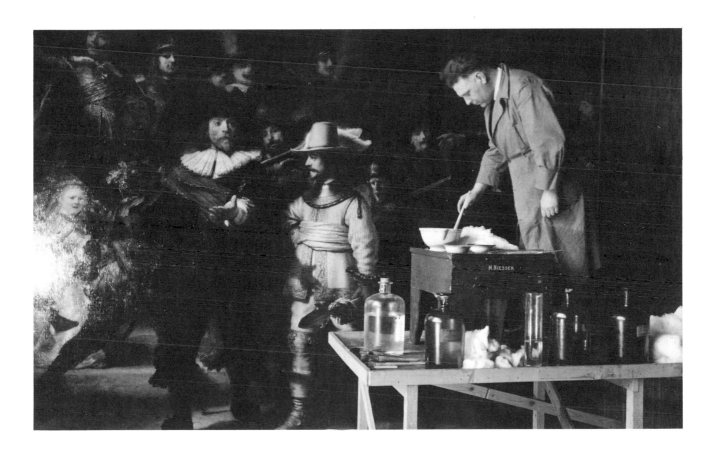

A hole in the drum was repaired before relining by the insertion of a new piece of canvas. That place too was then filled up with stopping.

The *Nightwatch* has now been given a coat of varnish. On this first layer of varnish the retouching will be done, so that it can easily be removed later, should it prove necessary.

The restorer J.A. Hesterman, with his sons F.C. Hesterman and J.A. Hesterman at the 1911 restoration of the *Nightwatch*.

layer downwards and the stretcher was removed. Chalk lines were drawn on the canvas to mark a border about 25 centimeters wide where the old relining canvas had to be left in place for the time being, so that it would be possible to turn the picture over again. The old relining canvas could now be removed.

To everyone's relief that proved an easy task. The adhesion between the original and the relining canvas was not too firm, and in some places it had even disappeared altogether. There were three reasons for this. The first was the composition of the relining adhesive: wax, resin and Venice turpentine in a proportion of 5:4:1. It further appeared that the relining canvas used in 1947 was too thick: it had absorbed too much of the wax-resin mixture before it could penetrate to the original canvas: and finally it seems probable that as little heat and pressure as possible was used during relining in 1947 in order to spare the varnish layer. The relining canvas was loosened and pulled away in bands about ten centimetres wide, often with the aid of knives. It then appeared, happily, that no complications had arisen in the areas damaged in September.

The cuts that had thus been "laid bare" had now to be joined together again. Thanks to the constant relative humidity of 58% and the temperature of 19° C in the temporary studio, the fibres in the canvas along the knife cuts proved to have righted themselves. Moreover, the fact that the cuts had been pasted over with mulberry paper right at the very beginning had also had a favourable effect on the repair of the fibres. Any resin and wax still remaining in those places was now removed and a start could be made on the joins.

Misunderstandings often arose over this question of joining; many people thought that the restorers set to work here like surgeons with needle and thread. But there was no question of that, for it would have done irreparable damage to the paint on the front of the canvas. No, the joins were made with many hundreds of linen threads, which were dipped in thinned epoxy resin (synthetic resin) and then stuck crossways over the cuts in the canvas – a most fiddling job that

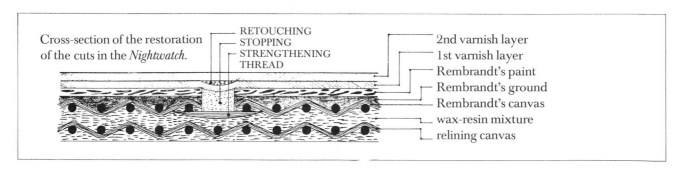

Cross-section of the restoration of the cuts in the *Nightwatch*.

RETOUCHING
STOPPING
STRENGTHENING THREAD

2nd varnish layer
1st varnish layer
Rembrandt's paint
Rembrandt's ground
Rembrandt's canvas
wax-resin mixture
relining canvas

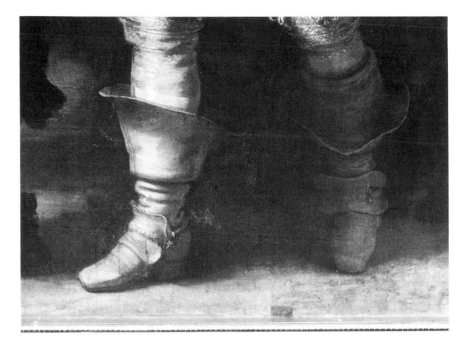

Van Ruytenburch's boot before restoration.

took no less than two whole weeks. All that time it had, of course, not been possible to see what the effect of this treatment was on the front of the painting, but now it was turned over and when the mulberry paper was pulled off the joins turned out to be good: they were smooth and regular and all that now remained to be seen of the horrifying scratches and cuts were whitish lines.

The removal of the protective mulberry paper did, however, give many visitors to the museum a big shock, for the damaged places then looked as if they had broken out in some horrible white rash. But for the professional this was nothing out of the ordinary: it was simply the effect of the paste on the varnish, which could be removed (by "regeneration") with 96% alcohol.

Because the cuts that had now been joined up felt like minuscule grooves by comparison with the rest of the surface of the painting, they had to be filled up with a flexible stopping. For this a mixture of chalk, raw umber and animal glue was used, slightly thinned with

When restoration work ceased for a time, the public in the Rijksmuseum could see through windows what stage had been reached.

The *Nightwatch* in its new glory. The painting has been varnished a second time and will have to hang for nearly a year in an enclosed space in order to allow the varnish to harden. During that time it can be seen through a glass wall.

Print of part of the X-ray photograph
made with sensitive material
– cronaflex – during the restoration.
The two repairs at the bottom are
clearly visible: an old restoration with
canvas of a different weave in Van
Ruytenburch's foot and a new
stopping under Banning Cocq's foot.
The photograph also gives an idea of
the changes Rembrandt himself made
in his painting: alterations in the
spontoon, in Van Ruytenburch's foot
and in the gorget under Banning
Cocq's white collar. On p.117 the same
detail on an ordinary photograph.

117

The shield with the names on an infra-red photograph of the *Nightwatch* itself (right).

Opinions differ somewhat as to the authenticity of the shield with the names on the *Nightwatch,* but it is at any rate clear that the names on the shield are not by Rembrandt's hand. It has also been assumed that the shield itself was not painted by Rembrandt, but added later. The evidence adduced for this is that on the infra-red photographs made of the shield in 1946 the architecture of the gateway can be seen running through under the shield. Another piece of evidence was to be found in the fact that there is no shield to be seen on the copy of the *Nightwatch* commonly attributed to Gerrit Lundens. However, on an infra-red photograph of the copy made in 1953 it can plainly be seen that the shield did appear on it originally, but that it was later painted over, the architecture painted over it being different in construction from that under the shield in Rembrandt's *Nightwatch.* Thus the painter of the copy must have known that there was a shield on the *Nightwatch,* but decided to remove it, for reasons which can no longer be discovered. So the copy no longer provides evidence to support the theory that the shield was a later addition. Moreover, in the microscopical examination during the 1975-6 restoration it was discovered that the grey colour which is used in the shield also crops up in the architecture to the right of it, reason enough to assume that architecture and shield were painted at the same time and thus are both the products of Rembrandt's hand.

Mention is sometimes made of the names of the sitters in a group portrait on the frame of the painting and sometimes, too, the painter himself tried to introduce the names into his picture in an inventive way, *e.g.* on a piece of paper painted to look as if it had been casually set down somewhere. It seems to be in the spirit of Rembrandt to inscribe those names on a shield that occupies a logical place in the picture.

turpentine oil. This was also the moment when the painting could be examined all over for weak places. Insertions, which, to judge from the paint, must have been applied over a hundred years ago, were checked against X-ray photographs. Some of them had to be replaced: a hole in the drum, for example, because the threads in the canvas of the old repair did not run parallel to those in Rembrandt's canvas, and a piece at the bottom because it had not been accurately applied and was badly joined.

When all this had been done, the moment arrived when the painting had to be relined. It had, therefore, to be turned over again, but that could not be done until the whole of the surface and more had been pasted over with strongly absorbent paper. This paper had a dual function: it served to support the picture while it was being turned over and it would be able to absorb any of the wax-resin adhesive that penetrated too deeply during relining. To this end a large wooden frame or loom was placed round the painting and the bands of paper, which were 1.40 metres wide, were carried over and stuck to it. Meanwhile, the work floor had been given an extra springy surface in the form of cork linoleum, this being necessary in order to protect the impasto on the paint layer during the ironing in of the wax-resin mixture that was to stick the new relining canvas to the original canvas.

At the back of that original canvas there was still a thick layer of wax and resin from the previous relining. This had to come off, of course, and that was done partly with xylene and partly by scraping with a knife. This loosened some old insertions and these were replaced by new ones, which were joined in by the same method as that used earlier on the cuts.

The shield with the names on an infra-red photograph of the copy of the *Nightwatch* (p.118, right).

The shield with the names on the *Nightwatch* used as a model for the memorial tablet on the place where Rembrandt is buried in the Westerkerk.

The relining itself was a far from easy and extremely nerveracking task. The new canvas, a single piece with no join, was first stretched on to a specially made relining frame that fitted inside the loom into which the painting had been pasted. Then it was carefully placed on the back of the painting and the adhesive mixture was brought up to the required temperature (around 68° C). It was a mixture of beeswax *(cera flava)* and natural resin (colophony) in a proportion of 5:2. Three big saucepansful were needed, each containing 2 kilograms of wax and 800 grams of resin. It was applied quickly to the canvas with large brushes and then ironed in with warm irons. The work went well and swiftly and at last the painting could be cut out of the loom and the relining frame could be turned over. When the paper was pulled away (dry) a "foggy" *Nightwatch* came into view, just as had been the case in the areas covered with mulberry paper, but this "fog" could be got rid of by a light brushing with alcohol, whereby the painting acquired its old, somewhat yellowed aspect again.

Now the old varnish had to be removed. That of 1947 disappeared on treatment with a solution of two parts alcohol and one part acetone, but the older varnish layers presented the restorers with a more difficult problem. They first had to be soaked with a thickened yellow turpentine, which could not evaporate quickly. Then, once they had become soft, they could be removed with a solution of two parts alcohol and two parts acetone. When that had been done, some rather worn places came to light, the presence of which had already been suspected by the experts. They were primarily to be found in nearly all the faces, which had probably been cleaned more often in the past than the rest of the canvas, a canvas which now looked so

Like other paintings, the *Nightwatch* has also undergone various "restorations" over the centuries. In 1678, for instance, Jan Smit treated the backs of a number of paintings with boiled oil and although the *Nightwatch* is not specifically mentioned by name on this occasion, it seems very likely that it also underwent this treatment. As for the reasons behind the treatment, they are not entirely clear, but it was perhaps thought that it would help to prevent the paint side of the picture from becoming dull, on the theory that there ought to be a balance between the layers applied on both sides of the painting.

In 1715 there is a first indication of the *Nightwatch* having been cleaned. In 1758 the shield with the names was discovered during cleaning and between 1850 and 1946 the painting was regenerated several times. The aim of all this was to make the varnish layer, which had become dull and opaque, transparent again.

The varnish used in 1947 was compounded on a basis of mastic resin. Various different sorts of resin are used in the making of varnish, such as dammar, copal, sandarac, etc. Mastic is a resin (in the form of tears) that quickly yellows, a drawback common to many natural resins if they remain in the dark for a long time. In addition mastic loses a great deal of its strength after a few years. If old layers of varnish are not completely removed, but are covered with a new layer, then the adhesion between them will naturally leave much to be desired and after some years the new layer will begin to crack, with the result that if one eventually wants to remove this unavoidable damage to the new surface, the cracking leads to powdering.

dull and dead that it was given a thin, temporary coat of varnish, so that the public would still be able to see at least something of the *Nightwatch* behind the glass wall during the Christmas holiday. After the holiday the temporary varnish was removed again and replaced by what is known as the retouching varnish. The application of this is a question of principle. One of the basic axioms of modern restoration practice is that retouched ("repainted") areas must not be able to adhere to the original paint of a picture. It must be possible for them to be easily removed, should ideas about retouching change in the future or should the areas become discoloured. If an extremely thin layer of varnish is applied to the original paint layer and the retouching is painted on this, then it will disappear when the varnish is dissolved. That is, some think nowadays, the most honest way of working and one that will not confront future generations with insurmountable problems.

And so the old and new areas of damage and the worn places were touched in with a rapidly drying oil paint, from which most of the oil had been removed. It was not a paint such as Rembrandt would have used, for that can no longer be copied, but ordinary good modern paint of various sorts, applied with thin sable brushes. Meanwhile an X-ray photograph had been made by night in accordance with a technique never used in the Netherlands before. Up to then X-ray pictures had generally been taken in the traditional manner with small sheets of sensitive material, but shortly before the *Nightwatch* was damaged, the Institut Royal du Patrimoine Artistique in Brussels had developed a new way of working. In this use is made of long bands of sensitive material 1.06 metres wide. Five of these bands were stretched vertically over the *Nightwatch*, so as to cover the entire painting. Then, in a single operation, the photograph was made from a distance of ten metres and with an exposure time of something over fifty minutes. The result was staggering: exceptionally sharp, highly "readable" and of the greatest possible value as a document for the future.

The end of the restoration was now rapidly approaching. After retouching, a few more inequalities in the edges of the painting were made good and finally, on 4 May 1976, the final coat of varnish was applied. Because this varnish dries very slowly and can easily develop a "bloom" from the breath of the public before it is completely dry, the Rijksmuseum had to decide to allow the painting to dry in a properly conditioned area, an area in which as far as possible the temperature would be kept at 19° C at a relative humidity of about 40%. This process will take about a year, a year in which the *Nightwatch* will thus be visible only behind a large glass wall. A "new" *Nightwatch*, many will say – at all events, a *Nightwatch* that is lighter in colour than it has ever been possible to see it in past centuries, a new light that probably comes closest to Rembrandt's original light of 1642.

Animal glue – an adhesive prepared from animal skins and bones.

Balsam – a soft, semi-liquid resin containing oil.

Bloom – a bluish film formed on the surface of a painting as a result of an excess of moisture in the atmosphere.

Boiled oil – oil whose drying properties have been improved by heating.

Colophony – resin with a low melting point, often used in combination with wax as an adhesive in the relining of paintings.

Copal – a rather hard type of resin with a high melting point, formerly much used in varnish.

Cradling – an arrangement of laths at the back of a panel to prevent it from warping.

Dammar – an East Indian type of resin, used in varnish and in combination with wax as an adhesive in relining.

Ground – the layer applied to the support to serve as a basis for painting on.

Impasto – paint applied in fairly thick layers, in which the brush strokes can sometimes be seen.

Infra-red examination – the effect of the heat of the infra-red rays gives an image of layers of paint deeper down. So that these can be seen, the work of art is photographed with material sensitive to infra-red radiation.

Loom – a wooden auxiliary frame used to support a painting during relining.

Mastic – a fragile, brittle type of resin in the form of tears, with a low melting point, much used in compounding varnishes.

Microphotograph – an enlargement of a photograph taken through a microscope.

Mulberry paper – thin Japanese paper made from mulberry bark.

Oil paint – dry pigment mixed with drying oil.

Powdering – the removal of an old varnish layer by means of reducing the top layer to powder by rubbing.

Raking light – a bright light directed at a painting from the side so that impasto casts a shadow, used in photographing paintings for restoration purposes.

Regeneration – making an existing varnish layer transparent again.

Relative humidity – the amount of water vapour present in the air at a given temperature in proportion to the maximum possible amount that could be present at that temperature. The relative humidity desirable in picture galleries is 55% at a temperature of 20° C.

Relining – the application with the aid of an adhesive of a new canvas to the back of an old one to strengthen it.

Retouching – the painting in of missing parts of a picture.

Resin – a sticky secretion given off primarily by pine or fir trees.

Sandarac – a hard type of resin, the basis of some types of varnish.

Stopping – a flexible putty composed of chalk, raw umber and animal glue, used to fill up holes in a painting; an area so filled.

Stretcher – a wooden framework with a sliding construction at the corners, on which the canvas is stretched. In each corner there are two wooden wedges, by means of which the stretcher can be extended.

Support – panel or canvas on which the ground, paint layer and varnish layer are applied.

Transfer – the removal of the old support and the application of the ground and paint layer to a new support.

Turpentine – a distillate from the balsam from which colophony resin is also made.

Turpentine substitute – a distillate from petroleum.

Ultra-violet examination – the work of art is irradiated with an ultra-violet lamp. This irradiation of a varnish layer can make it possible to see any parts of a painting that are missing or were added later.

Umber – a dark-brown earth pigment with iron- and manganese-oxides.

Varnish – resin dissolved in turpentine or turpentine substitute, used to give a final coat to a painting to protect it and to bring out the colours to better advantage.

Venice turpentine – balsam from the larch tree.

X-ray photograph – the work of art is exposed to X-rays, which are absorbed by paint containing lead. Thanks to this, the innermost parts of a painting can be made visible on special photographic material.

Xylene (or xylol) – a distillate from petroleum, used to degrease the front or back of a painting.

Chronology

Key dates in the life of Rembrandt Harmenszoon van Rijn

1606	Rembrandt born on 15 July at Leiden, the son of Harmen Gerritsz. van Rijn (d. 1630) and Neeltje van Suydtbroek (d. 1640)
1613	goes to the Latin School in Leiden
1620	enrolment as a student in the letters faculty of Leiden University
c. 1621-4	learns the principles of the art of painting under the Leiden painter Jacob van Swanenburch (c. 1571-1638)
1624-5	works for six months in Amsterdam under the history painter Pieter Lastman (1583-1633), who has a great influence on him
1625-31	working as an independent painter in Leiden; close co-operation with his friend Jan Lievens (1607-74)
1628-31	Gerard Dou (1613-67) is Rembrandt's first pupil
1629-30	in his autobiography Constantijn Huygens writes of Rembrandt (among other things): "For I maintain, that no .... Apelles .... could have imagined .... what a young man, a Dutchman, a beardless miller's son has summed up and expressed in a single figure: bravo Rembrandt!"
1631	in the autumn settles for good in Amsterdam, where he lives in the house of the art dealer Hendrick van Uylenburgh in Sint Anthonies Breestraat (now Jodenbreestraat); up to about 1635 Govert Flinck, Ferdinand Bol and Jan Victors are his most important pupils
1634	marries Saskia van Uylenburgh (1612-42), a cousin of Hendrick van Uylenburgh, at Sint Annaparochie (Friesland) on 22 June
1636	birth of Rumbartus, who dies after two months; removal to Nieuwe Doelenstraat; up to about 1640 Gerbrandt van den Eeckhout is his most important pupil
1638	birth of Cornelia (1), who dies within a month
1639	buys a house in Sint Anthonies Breestraat (the Rembrandthuis, 4-6 Jodenbreestraat)
1640	birth of Cornelia (2), who dies within a month; up to about 1645 Carel Fabritius, Samuel van Hoogstraten, Lambert Doomer and Jurriaen Ovens are his most important pupils
1641	birth of Titus (d. 1668)
1642	Saskia dies in June
1643-9	Geertge Dircks (d. 1656?) lives in Rembrandt's house; up to about 1655 Nicolaes Maes, Barent Fabritius and Willem Drost are his most important pupils
c. 1649	Hendrickje Stoffels (c. 1626-63) takes Geertge's place
1654	in July Hendrickje is reprimanded by the Church Council for her sinful way of life; in October Cornelia (3) is born
1656	*cessio bonorum* on account of debts; an inventory made in July of Rembrandt's possessions
1657	first sale of possessions
1658	sales of the house and further possessions
1660	Rembrandt has moved to Rozengracht, Hendrickje and Titus run an art-dealing business in order to keep the family's income at a reasonable level; around 1661 Aert van Gelder becomes Rembrandt's pupil; he continues to work in the manner of his master up to his death in 1727
1663	death of Hendrickje Stoffels
1668	in February Titus marries Magdalena van Loo (d. 1669); in September Titus dies
1669	in March Rembrandt's granddaughter Titia (d. 1725) is born; on 4 October Rembrandt dies; on 8 October he is buried in the Westerkerk; a few days later Magdalena, Titus' widow, dies

Bibliography

On Rembrandt

K. Clark, *Rembrandt and the Italian Renaissance,* London 1966
R.H. Fuchs, *Rembrandt in Amsterdam,* Greenwich, Connecticut, 1968
H. Gerson, *Rembrandt Paintings,* Amsterdam, 1968
B. Haak, *Rembrandt,* New York, 1969
J. Rosenberg, *Rembrandt, Life and Work,* London, 1964
S. Slive, *Rembrandt and his Critics, 1630-1730,* The Hague, 1953
S. Slive, *Drawings of Rembrandt,* 2 Vols., New York, 1965
H. van de Waal, *Steps Towards Rembrandt,* Amsterdam, 1974
C. White, *Rembrandt and his World,* London, 1963

On the Nightwatch

H. Gerson, *Rembrandt: La Ronde de Nuit, Rijksmuseum,* Fribourg 1973
T. Koot, *Rembrandt's Nightwatch: a Fascinating Story,* Amsterdam, 1969

On restoration

L. Kuiper, *Restoration of Paintings,* Bussum 1975
G.L. Stout, *The Care of Pictures,* Columbia University Press, 1948
H. Ruheman, *The Cleaning of Paintings,* London, 1968

On restorations of the Nightwatch

A. van Schendel and H.H. Mertens, "De restauratie van Rembrandt's Nachtwacht", *Oud Holland* 62, 1947, pp. 1 ff. English summary pp. 49-52
"The Restoration of Rembrandt's *Nightwatch*", *Bulletin van het Rijksmuseum* 24, 1976, Nos. 1 & 2, parallel texts in Dutch and English

On Dutch art

J. Rosenberg, S. Slive, E.H. ter Kuile, *Dutch Art and Architecture 1600 to 1800,* Pelican History of Art, 1966
Art in Seventeenth Century Holland, exhibition catalogue, National Gallery, London, 1976
All the Paintings in the Rijksmuseum. A completely illustrated catalogue by the Department of Paintings of the Rijksmuseum, Amsterdam/Maarssen, 1976

On Amsterdam and the Republic

P. Burke, *Venice and Amsterdam. A Study of seventeenth-century élites,* London, 1974
P. Geyl, *The Revolt of the Netherlands,* London, 1966
The Netherlands in the Seventeenth Century, Parts 1 and 2, London, 1961 and 1964
K. Fremantle, *The Baroque Town Hall of Amsterdam,* Utrecht, 1959
J.H. Huizinga, *Dutch Civilization in the 17th Century,* London, 1968
J.L. Price, *Culture and Society in the Dutch Republic During the 17th Century,* London, 1974
C. Wilson, *The Dutch Republic,* London, 1968

Index

List of illustrations

32. Claes Jansz. Visscher (c. 1589-1660), *Plan of Amsterdam*, c. 1650. Photograph: Historisch Topografische Atlas, Amsterdam.

33 Paulus van Hilligaert (1595/6-1640), *The Siege of 's Hertogenbosch*, 1629. Amsterdam. Rijksmuseum / / Receipt of the Dutch East India Company, published in 1606. Amsterdam, Historisch Archief van de Vereniging voor de Effectenhandel

34 *The House of Safety on Nova Zembla*, from Gerrit de Veer, *Van drie Seylagien ter werelt noyt soo vreemt ghehoort*, Amsterdam, 1598 / / Reinier Nooms, called Zeeman (c. 1623-before 1667), *Guardhouse or Chamber of the Commissioners of Maritime Affairs*, from *Verscheyde Schepen en Gesichten van Amstelredam*

35 Willem Schellincks (1627-78), *The Breach in St. Anthony's Dyke near Houtewael, 5 March 1651*. Amsterdam, Historical Museum / / Rembrandt, *The Quack Doctor*, drawing, c. 1637. London, Private collection.

36 Debenture issued by the Polder Board of Lekdijk Bovendams in 1638. Amsterdam, Historisch Archief van de Vereniging voor de Effectenhandell Unknown artist, *The City Orphanages for Boys and Girls in Amsterdam*. Photograph: Stedelijk Museum, Amsterdam.

37 Rembrandt, *The Rat-catcher*, etching, 1632 / / Rembrandt, *Street Musicians*, etching, c. 1633. Rembrandt, *The Pedlar, etching, 1636* / / Rembrandt, *Beggar with Wooden Leg*, etching, c. 1630.

38 Emanuel de Witte (1616/17-92), *The New Fish Market in Amsterdam*. Amsterdam, Rijksmuseum (c. 1677?) / / Job Berckheyde (1630-93), *The Inside of the Amsterdam Stock Exchange*. Amsterdam, Historical Museum, after 1668 / / Jan van der Heyden (1637-1712), *The Dam at Amsterdam with the Nieuwe Kerk*. Amsterdam, Historical Museum

39 Jan Tengnagel (1584/5-1635), *Seventeen Militiamen of the Handbow Archers'* Doelen, 1613. Amsterdam, Rijksmuseum, on loan from the City of Amsterdam

40 Weapons from the General Hoefer Army Museum, Leiden. The Musket below is the property of the Rijksmuseum, Amsterdam.

41 Stone tablet from the façade of the *Kloveniersdoelen* in Amsterdam. Amsterdam, Historical museum / / *To the Noble Fraternity of the Militia Order of St. Michael*, poem published by Thomas Fontein, Amsterdam, 1659. Amsterdam, Doelen Hotel / / Chest from *Kloveniersdoelen* in Amsterdam, 1639. Amsterdam, Historical Museum.

42 Gerard van Honthorst (1590-1656), *Maria de Medicis*, 1639. Amsterdam, Historical Museum / / Salomon Savery (c. 1594-after 1664) after J. Martsen the Younger, *The Triumphal Arch on the Vijgendam at the Entry of Maria de Medicis on 1 September 1638*, from Caspar Barlaeus, *Medicea Hospes*, 1638. Rotterdam, Atlas van Stolk

43 Jacob de Gheyn (1565-1629), *Wapen-handelinghe van roers, musquetten ende spiessen*, Amsterdam 1608 / / Bartholomeus van der Helst (1613-70), *The Four Doelheren of the Handbow Doelen in 1653*, 1657 Amsterdam, Rijksmuseum, on loan from the City of Amsterdam

44 The chain of the *Kloveniers'* Guild of Amsterdam, first quarter of the 16th century. Amsterdam, Historical Museum / / Thomas de Keyser (1596/7 1667), *The Company of Captain Jacob Symonsz. de Vries and Lieutenant Dirck de Graeff*, 1633. Amsterdam. Historical Museum

45 Jan van Bijlert (1597-1671), *The Sutler*, c. 1640, Utrecht, Central Museum / / Drinking horn of the *Kloveniers'* Guild of Amsterdam, 1547. Amsterdam, Rijksmuseum, on loan from the City of Amsterdam

46 Rembrandt, *The* Swijgh Utrecht *Tower*, drawing, 1652-3. Amsterdam, Rijksprenten-kabinet / / Abraham Rademaker (1675-1735), *The Doelen Tower in Amsterdam in 1607*, print, from *Nederlandsche Outheeden en Gezigten*. Photograph: Historisch Topografische Atlas, Amsterdam

47 Jan Ekels (1724-81), *The* Kloveniersdoelen *on the Amstel Side*, 1775. Amsterdam, Historical Museum.

49 *Specie Book Containing the Computation of Many Gold and Silver Coins*, Amsterdam, title-page and pp. 42-3. Amsterdam, Historisch Archief van de Vereniging voor de Effectenhandel / / Seventeenth-century coins. The Hague, Royal Cabinet of Coins, Medals and Gems

50 Jacob Adriaensz. Backer, *Portrait of an Unknown Man*, probably a self portrait. Lyon Museum / / Jacob Adriaensz. Backer, *The Company of Captain Cornelis de Graeff and Lieutenant Hendrick Lauwrensz.*, 1642. Amsterdam, Rijksmuseum, on loan from the City of Amsterdam.

51 Govert Flinck, *Self Portrait*. Whereabouts unknown / / Govert Flinck, *The Company of Captain Albert Bas and Lieutenant Lucas Conijn*, 1645. Amsterdam. Rijksmuseum, on loan from the City of Amsterdam / / Govert Flinck, *The four Governors of the Arquebusiers' Civic Guard*, 1642. Amsterdam, Rijksmuseum, on loan from the City of Amsterdam

52 Rembrandt, *The Nightwatch*, before the restoration of 1975-6. Amsterdam, Rijksmuseum, on loan from the City of Amsterdam.

54 Joachim von Sandrart, *The Company of Captain Cornelis Bicker and Lieutenant Frederick van Banchem*, 1638. Amsterdam, Rijksmuseum, on loan from the city of Amsterdam

55 Nicolaes Eliasz., called Pickenoy, *The Company of Captain Jan Claesz. Vlooswijck and Lieutenant Gerrit Hudde*, 1642. Amsterdam, Rijksmuseum, on loan from the City of Amsterdam

56 Rembrandt, *The Nightwatch*, after the restoration of 1975-6. Amsterdam, Rijksmuseum, on loan from the City of Amsterdam.

58 Bartholomeus van der Helst, *The Company of Captain Roelof Bicker and Lieutenant Jan Michielsz. Blaeuw*, 1639. Amsterdam, Rijksmuseum, on loan from the City of Amsterdam

60 Frans Hals (1580-1666), *The Officers of the St. George's* Doelen *in Haarlem*, 1616. Haarlem, Frans Hals Museum

62 Attributed to Gerrit Lundens (1622-after 1683) *Copy of the* Nightwatch. Amsterdam, Rijksmuseum, on loan from the National Gallery, London / / Jacob Cats (1741-99), *Copy after the "Lundens" copy of the* Night-watch, watercolour, 1779. Amsterdam, Rijksprentenkabinet / / L.A. Claessens, 1763-1834, *Copy of the* Nightwatch, engraving, 1797